Dead Cocks Don't Crow

———⋈———

J S COWEN

Dead Cock's Don't Crow

Author – Jenny S Cowen

© Jenny S Cowen 2024

All rights reserved. No part of this publication may not be reproduced in whole or part, stored, posted on the internet, or transmitted in any form or by any means, electronic, mechanical, photocopying, recording, or other, without permission from the author of this book.

This book is a biography based on both documented historical facts and personal accounts. While every effort has been made to ensure the accuracy of the information contained herein, the author and publisher make no representations or warranties regarding the completeness or accuracy of the content. The book is intended for educational and informational purposes only and should not be considered definitive.

The photographs included in this book have been sourced from public archives, personal collections, and other available resources. All efforts have been made to identify and credit the rightful owners of these images. If any photograph has been used inadvertently without proper credit or permission, please contact the publisher so that the necessary corrections can be made in subsequent editions.

Typeset and cover design by BookPOD

ISBN: 978-0-9945173-4-0 (pbk)   eISBN: 978-0-9945173-5-7 (e-book)

 A catalogue record for this book is available from the National Library of Australia

Author's Note

I became acquainted with Thomas Toke when I was a law undergraduate at Melbourne University. Dr Ruth Campbell gave me the case of Crown versus Chamberlain and Armstrong to investigate as part of the subject known then as "Legal History". My sixth-sense made me suspicious of Toke. I began to keep notes on him. On completion of my degree my investigation into Toke began in earnest. I had no idea then, that it would take me the best part of forty years to publish Toke's story.

Initially I received support and encouragement in my endeavours from my family and a small circle of friends. Mrs Betty Malone OA, checked facts for me and located obscure sources. My Father, Sister and a close friend, Laurie Curry gave up weekends and joined me in the La Trobe Library, in Melbourne, to help in my research.

The people of Omeo and in particular their Historical Society members, including Dianne Carroll, Jeff Cooper, Max Dyer and Vic Webber searched records and provided material. They also gave me their insights into the area.

The La Trobe Library (as it was then known, now the Public Record Office Victoria) and its staff members were my mainstay. Without their commitment and willingness to search their records it is doubtful that this book could ever have been written.

Thank goodness for the Internet. This modern marvel has enabled me to complete the book without leaving home and has allowed me to communicate with many libraries and institutions.

My main aim in publishing Toke's life is to prove that history is not dead. There is a plethora of life stories waiting to be told. Many, like Toke's co-exist with the major events in the history of countries and societies. They reflect the life-styles and attitudes of the time and if heeded may guide us to a greater understanding of our own lives and times. I also wished to expose some of the travesties of justice that occurred in the nineteenth centuries. I cannot rectify those travesties, but hopefully some of the individuals mentioned in my book will be forgiven and or given their rightful place in history.

Finally, this book had to be written. Thomas Toke stands here. Read his life story. I am sure you will agree with me, he must be held accountable for his crimes.

J. S. Cowen LLB

Contents

Prologue 1

England 3

Transportation 9

Sydney Town 17

Port Phillip 23

Port Arthur 37

Oatlands 45

Norfolk Island 51

Port Arthur Re-visited 57

Gold and Freedom 59

Mewburn Park, Victoria 65

Livingstone Creek, Omeo 71

Life and Litigation in Omeo 1858-1859 95

Mr Cornelius Green and the Case for Gold Escorts 101

Planning and Executing a Gold Robbery 109

Apprehension of the Murderers 113

R-v- George Chamberlain and William Armstrong	121
A Marriage of Convenience	131
Politics and the issue of Law and Order	135
The Second Trial, of Chamberlain and Armstrong.	141
Armstrong's Confession	159
The Aftermath	167
Pay Back Time	179
1863	183
The Tichborne Case	195
Pentridge and Beyond	205
Land	209
Mr Thomas Toke Landowner	219
The Aftermath of Toke's Death	227
The Twentieth Century	235
Conclusion	239
Index	241

Prologue

You fools, you think that you know all about your past, you sit on your computers and tap into all types of information; and yet you will not find me there. I am far more infamous than your Ned Kelly, what was he but a "seven day wonder". Ned killed, but couldn't evade a meagre police force hell bent on his capture. That police force even turned to me for assistance in locating his tracks and hideouts in country Victoria.

Who am I? I am Thomas Toke, alias Thomas Tookey, alias Thomas Toak. I was born in England, transported to Sydney, Australia and endured all the hellholes of incarceration that the new Colonies could supply and I survived. No hangman's noose for me, I murdered my fair share of individuals, I stole horses (all of them grey coloured and sound), I blackmailed and terrorised whole communities and I died of natural causes. You don't believe me, you think I boast, well, you read my tale and then see what you think.

England

I was born in Newmarket Street, London, England in the year 1811, I do not know the exact date, as no one bothered to note this auspicious occasion. My father, Thomas Toke was a butcher and my mother Elizabeth Sarah, nee Smith well who was she? Did she care about her son I don't know. Did I have brothers or sisters, I don't know. All I know was that I was a cast off, sent to live with my betters at Godinton Park on the outskirts of Ashford in Kent. I spent my early years there with the genteel members of my family learning to read and write, and to ride. I had the family history forced down my gullet. My relatives were forever reminding me that Godinton Park had been the seat of the Toke family since 1440. My family was an ancient one. The Toke's, reputed to be descended from Sieur de Touques, may have fought at the Battle of Hastings. We were definitely related to Robert de Toke who was present at the Battle of Northampton in 1264.[1] Are you interested in this twaddle? I was not. I was never going to be mentioned in the illustrious family history, all I was was a by-blow of some distant relative who was taken in out of charity and who was continually reminded of his standing in the family.

---

1   Godinton Park by Christopher Hussey,C.B.E,F.S.A.

Godinton Park

I did not appreciate the great hall, the gallery, the dining rooms and libraries. These were not the haunts of a small lad who was not to inherit any part of the family fortune. I endured my hard and long lessons in that house, and I learnt them well. I could read and write better than any of my peers and I could ride. Yes I did love the park at Godinton, which was studded with many great trees. I could escape the confines of the house and the continuous and long-winded lectures, I could ride for hours and enjoy my own company; the house and family meant nothing to me.

At the age of fifteen I was summoned to my Uncle's library and in his snobbish and effected voice delivered yet another boring diatribe; in this speech however I was told that I was to find my own way in the world. My family had educated, fed and housed me, now I was on my own "the world was my oyster", with hard work and the fear of the Lord I could achieve great things. It was made patently clear to me that I was not welcome to return to Godinton unless I made something of myself. With that I was shown the door.

For all their posturing and all the past glories, Godinton Park did not remain in the Toke family's possession for much longer. The property was sold in the 1890's, the Toke's were without property for the first time in centuries, but I had my patch far removed from England and far removed from all company save for my faithful pack of dogs.

So in 1825 I was on my own. I was not initially prepared for the harsh realities of nineteenth century England. If you cannot imagine the scene go read a Charles Dicken's novel and you will see what I was up against. I was fifteen for Christ's sake, how was I going to earn an honest living? No, why should I earn an honest living? So I took some food, and got caught, but I cried poor and the Court took pity on me, especially with my affliction. Did I tell you I had what is described in polite company as a speech impediment? I stutter, and it is not an affliction, I learnt to use my stutter to my advantage. Establishment thought I was dumb, so I let them think I was. A poor young stuttering fool didn't know better, next time I stole I was more adept at it, but I was still caught. I was brought up before the Magistrate, and convicted of larceny. My sentence of one month's imprisonment was a blessing. I had accommodation, of a sort, during the cold weather of early 1826 and I learnt all manner of skills from my new peers. I looked forward to my release and to using my new skills in my career as a petty criminal.

On my release I teamed up with George Brassington, he was deaf and I stuttered. I thought we would make a great team, but George was slow and we got nabbed for stealing two loaves of bread. Yes we were your stereotype poor lads. So hungry we were forced to steal our food, how pitiful! Not true, we stole what we wanted, why should we work when we could take what we needed? We were young and confident.

I.S. 6

CONVICT RECORDS

Name of Convict: George Brassington.

A. **Convict Indent** for the Ship: Bussorah Merchant   AO NSW ref. 4/4013
Port and date of Departure: England   COD
Date of arrival: 26 July 1828   Reel 398

Name	: George Brassington.	Hair colour: Dark brown
Age	: 17 Years.	Eye colour: Hazel and Full.
Education	: None.	Marks or scars:
Religion	: Protestant.	Anchor nearly defaced on left arm, ring
Marital Status	: Single.	on middle finger of left hand, blue
No. of children	:	speck on right arm, deaf.
Native Place	: Greenwich.	
Trade or calling	: Fishermans Bay	
Offence	: Stealing 2 loaves of	
Where tried	: Kent bread.	
When tried	: 27 March 1826	How disposed of:
Sentence	: 7 Years.	Ticket of leave:
Former convictions	: None	Conditional Pardon:
Height	: 5'0½"	Absolute Pardon:
Complexion	: Ruddy, little dark	Certificate of Freedom: C 36/232
Remarks/ Disposed to	: James Mordant, Sydney.	

B. Ticket of Leave   AO NSW ref.4/   COD   Reel

Name:	Allowed to remain
Ticket of Leave No:	in district of:
Date of Ticket:	Bench making recommendation:
Remarks:	

ENGLAND

| C. Pardon | AO NSW ref. 4/ | COD | Reel |

Name:
Type of Pardon:
Remarks:

No. of Pardon:
Date of Pardon:

| D. Certificate of Freedom | AO NSW ref.4/ 4332 | COD | Reel 996 |

Name: George Brassington   Certificate No:36/232   Date: 11 April 1835
Remarks: "Was transported tp Moreton Bay for three years by the Parramatta Bench, 28 Dec 1830, for running away and robbing his master".

| E. 1828 Census | AO NSW ref. COD 245 |

Name: George Brassington

Children

Age: -
Free or bond: -
Ship: B. Merchant
Year: -
Sentence: -
Religion: -
Occupation: -
Employer/Remarks
   Road - Gang 20

| Name | Age | Free or Bond |

Residence:

Land and stock holdings:

Convicts sent to & from Moreton Bay (AO NSW: 4/3897), p: 32 listed George Brassington as a prisoner being transported to Moreton Bay on 3 February 1831 by the ship Governor Phillip.

Sources checked without success:

☐ Colonial Secretary Card Indexes
☐ Mutch Index to births, deaths and marriages (AO NSW ref:Reel   )
☐ Card index to Co. of Cumberland Bench of Magistrates hearings, 1788-1820
☐ Other Sources:

☐ Registers of permission to marry (AO NSW ref:)
☐ Indexes to land grants and leases (AO NSW ref:)
☐ Colonial Secretary: Index to letters received re land

George and I appeared before John D'Oyley, Sergeant at Law at the Kent December Assizes on Friday 31 March 1826. What a joke, so many of us poor misguided souls dragged before D'Oyley and his twelve jurors, some of the ninnies pleaded not guilty. The legal system didn't exist for the likes of us, so I pleaded guilty. I'd stolen the bread; I wasn't going to be hung for it. Brassington and I stood trial in Maidstone, Kent, and the 'beak' convicted us and sentenced both George and me to seven years transportation.[2]

---

2   Kent December Assizes – March 31,1826

Transportation

According to my official Convict Record, although I can't remember what I was like back then, I was fifteen years of age, four feet nine and a half inches tall with dark brown hair and chestnut coloured eyes. I already had my tattoo, I was proud of it "ST" on my left arm and I had scares; one on my right eyebrow and one on the back of my left hand, these I sustained from the scrapes I had been in. Even then I was not pretty. The mole on the left side of my neck was noted and my sallow and pox pitted completion duly notated. So what, I was never going to be a ladies man.

I had given my calling as a "seaboy" and so I was off to sea, at His Majesty's expense. I, with all the other convicts were loaded like cattle onto the Bussorah Merchant in the port of London, bound for Sydney, New South Wales. This was the Bussorah Merchant's maiden voyage as a convict ship, a barque really, and if I had ever had the freedom of the ship I could have confirmed that it was one hundred and seventeen feet long and thirty one feet, eleven inches wide and five hundred and thirty ton. As ships go, she was quite a good-looking vessel, three-mast rig built entirely from teak at Calcutta in 1818. The Master of the vessel was

I.S. 6

CONVICT RECORDS

Name of Convict: Thomas Toke

A. **Convict Indent** for the Ship: Bussorah Merchant   AO NSW ref.4/4013
    Port and date of Departure: England   COD
    Date of arrival: 26 July 1828   Reel 398

Name	: Thomas Toke	Hair colour: Dark brown
Age	: 15 years	Eye colour: Chestnut
Education	: Read	Marks or scars:
Religion	: Protestant	Mole on left side of neck; scar on
Marital Status	: Single	right eyebrow; ST on left arm; scar
No. of children	: -	on back of left hand; has impediment
Native Place	: Kent	in his speech.
Trade or calling	: Seaboy	
Offence	: Stealing 2 loaves of bread	
Where tried	:	
When tried	: 27 March 1826	How disposed of:
Sentence	: 7 years	Ticket of leave:
Former convictions	: 2 years	Conditional Pardon:
Height	: 4'9½"	Absolute Pardon:
Complexion	: Sallow, pox pitted	Certificate of Freedom: C.33/662
Remarks	:	

B. Ticket of Leave   AO NSW ref.4/   COD   Reel

Name:
Ticket of Leave No: Allowed to remain
Date of Ticket: in district of:
Remarks: Bench making recommendation:

TRANSPORTATION

C. Pardon   AO NSW ref. 4/   COD   Reel

Name: No. of Pardon:
Type of Pardon: Date of Pardon:
Remarks:

D. Certificate of Freedom   AO NSW ref.4/ 4316   COD   Reel 991

Name: Thomas Toke   Certificate No: 33/662   Date: 19 June 1833
Remarks:
           "15 years, Melbourne Quarter Sessions, 15 Sep. 1841"

E. 1828 Census   AO NSW ref. COD 245

Name: | Children
Age: | Name   Age   Free or Bond
Free or bond:
Ship:
Year:
Sentence:
Religion:
Occupation:
Employer/Remarks

Residence: No entry

Land and stock holdings:

Sources checked without success:
  ☐ Colonial Secretary Card Indexes
  ☐ Mutch Index to births, deaths and
    marriages (AO NSW ref:Reel   )
  ☐ Card index to Co. of Cumberland
    Bench of Magistrates hearings,
    1788-1820
  ☐ Other Sources:

  ☐ Registers of permission to
    marry (AO NSW ref:)
  ☐ Indexes to land grants and
    leases (AO NSW ref:)
  ☐ Colonial Secretary: Index
    to letters received re land

Bussorah Merchant

Mr Baigrie. Also on board were Surgeon Superintendent, Dr. R. Dunn, R.N; Captain Deveney, of the 57th Regiment; Ensign Child, of the 39th Regiment; one man of the 57th and 30 men of the 39th, who were our guards. Five women and six children also made the voyage.[3]

Smallpox appeared on board before we even sailed and a Negro seaman was removed to the hospital ship at Chatham. The authorities must have thought that the crew and all of us convicts had been vaccinated, as the ship was permitted to sail on 27th March 1828. Four cases of smallpox occurred during the passage, two of the patients were convicts but all four recovered.[4] I did not pine for England, the "mother-country", who was all too pleased to rid itself of the likes of me. I shared the one hundred and twenty one day journey with the other one hundred and sixty nine felons and did not see the sights or explore the ports we put in to on the way to our destination. We did not walk the decks or eat a whole day's rations. We were crammed into the hull with little opportunity to exercise. The stench of my companions was unbearable, I pledged that

---

3   Sydney Gazette-Shipping Intelligence 28 July 1828.
4   Charles Henry Bateson – The Covict Ships 1787-1868 p.252.

Transportation

I would not willingly tolerate being incarcerated again but I did make some interesting acquittances on that my first sea voyage.

We arrived in New South Wales on 26th July 1828, with only four convicts dying on the voyage. This apparently was considered a very good outcome. The smallpox outbreak was not reported when we arrived at Port Jackson because there had been no sign of the disease on board the vessel since early in May. Someone must have spilt the beans to the port authorities because they went into a mild panic. The "passengers" and crew were landed on a small beach at North Head, which was a remote and rugged promontory at the entry to Sydney Harbour. A small colonial vessel, the Alligator, was converted into a hospital. The only patients from the Bussorah Merchant were a few men suffering from minor ailments. The Bussorah Merchant's surgeon-superintendent, Robert Dunn, considered the precautions unnecessary. The people of Sydney did not according to newspaper reports:

> "The promptness which was manifested by the Government immediately on the arrival of the Bussorah Merchant, when the fact was ascertained that so severe a distemper as smallpox had been prevalent on board calls for the most fervent commendation of a deeply interested Community...Providence, we trust, effectually obstructed the introduction of so awful a distemper amongst us; for, we have no doubt, the utmost vigilance will be in exercised to see that the tenor of the Proclamation is enforced and obeyed. We are not sorry, in one sense, that the toxin has been so impressively sounded in our ears, as it will have the desired effect of compelling parents, and the guardians of our youth, from allowing the rising generation any longer to be exposed to the ravages of the small-pox, or in fact, to any other disease against which we have no means of providing. It is only four months since that the hooping cough found its way to the Colony on the Morley...

> Now the smallpox is come. We sincerely think it necessary, from the alarm which has penetrated every parent's bosom, to advise those of our fellow-Colonists, who are favored with such interesting pledges, to lose no time in getting them inoculated, though we are sorry to be informed, at this eventful crisis, that there is no vaccine virus in the Colony. We trust that this will turn our not to be the fact"[5]

The colonist were so terrified of us on the Bussorah Merchant that they even considered that the natives of the area might catch and carry the disease to their dear loved ones. None of us on board had at that stage seen an aboriginal but the authorities took great pains to ensure we did not meet:

> "...Boongarrie, the black chief, is actually in the pay of the Government to keep off the natives, who, on the other hand, are more fearful of the infection of such a disease perhaps than we ourselves; for, in the early stages of the Colony, the small-pox swept away the black population by hundreds, if not thousands. But this report is only another proof of what ingenuity is capable of devising, when under the influence of evil passions. His Excellency will ever be entitled to the best thanks of the Colonists for the paternal anxiety which he has evinced in the case of the Bussorah Merchant alone".[6]

During the period of quarantine, if any communication between the Bussorah Merchant and the colony, or any supplies were required, Captain Baigrie had to expend a pound and a half of powder, to attract attention. This activity was a distraction to this period of enforced boredom.[7]

---

5   Sydney Gazette July 30, 1828
6   Sydney Gazette, August 15, 1828
7   Sydney Gazette August 25, 1828

The ship received a favourable medical report on August 21, but was not released from quarantine until the following month.[8]

And what did the 'gentlemen' on board the Bussorah Merchant have to say about Captain Baigrie? The good Captain ensured that favourable letters found their way into the local press.

Sydney, July 27th 1828

"Sir – It is with much pleasure that I hand you this my certificate, expressive of the satisfaction I feel at the kind and liberal manner in which I have been treated since my embarkation on board the Bussorah Merchant; at the same time I cannot omit to thank you for the very generous and humane attention you have been pleased to pay to the wants of sick soldiers, women and children, of the guard, under my command, during their long and tedious passage from England to Sydney.

I am, Sir, your obedient humble servant,
Burton Daveney,
Capt. 57th Regt. Commanding on board"[9]

I was strong and had survived the journey, I did not care about the four souls who died on the voyage, no one had shown any sympathy for me chained and fettered in that stinking hull.

---

8   Charles Henry Bateson – The Convict ships – 1787-1868 p.252.
9   Sydney Gazette September 8,1828.

Sydney Town

My initial glimpse of Sydney was short and sweet, as I was disposed to Carters' Barracks. My new home was constructed in the illustrious reign of Governor Macquarie and was purpose built to house convict carters and brick-makers and of course, to accommodate the Government's horses and bullocks. I was sent to Carters' Barracks because it was a penitentiary for juvenile convicts. There I would be taught a useful trade.

I found myself in the boys' barracks, one hundred of us, separated from the other two hundred male convicts by a high wall with our own mess rooms and kitchens. Sounds good doesn't it? In reality we young ones were crowded into a small area with a sleeping space of fourteen square feet, with a three foot passage between the two rows of hammocks. I vowed then and there that when I was released from this hellhole I would never live in a town or city again.

So my salvation would be a trade. The Town Surveyors and Surveyor General's horses were stabled at the Barracks. I knew that I could ride and care for the horses better than the stable-hands and hoped that if I were forced to a trade it would be with horses. This was the last time that I put my faith in the establishment.

Dead Cocks Don't Crow

Adjoining the Barracks was a treadmill, the "climbing sorrow"[10] which was used for the purpose of correcting tarnished morals. I was deemed fractious and deceitful, so I was sent to the treadmill, to trudge a never-ending path on a wicked and unforgiving machine. A large treadmill circumference was eighteen feet eight inches. One revolution of the wheel took thirty seconds. There were sixty of us assigned to the large treadmill, eighteen men on the wheel at one time, with each team spending thirty-six minutes on the wheel and twenty-four minutes off. The steps of the wheel were about nine inches apart. Our hours of labour were sunrise to sunset, with of course one hour for dinner and about half an hour whilst we "adjusted" ourselves to the work. This meant that in winter we poor sods worked ten shifts and in summer eleven. All the backbreaking work was for the purpose of grinding and dressing grain. As for my daily rations at Carter's Barracks I received:

> 1lb of wheat meal ground entirely down, including the bran, or its produce in bread;
> 7/10 lbw.maize flour;
> 1lb beef or 4/7lb salt pork;
> 1 1/7oz. sugar;
> 1/2oz. salt.

Breakfast at the Barracks consisted of maize flour made into gruel or stir-about. Dinner was soup and boiled meat with vegetables from the garden at the Barracks.[11]

My spirit would not be broken, I suffered and toiled and on Sunday's heard the never-ending litany of do-good clergy. I was a survivor and despite

---

10 Newspaper cuttings Vol 116 p 109, Mitchell Library
11 Extracts from the Report of the Committee on the Subject of Treadwheel Labour October 1825, Mitchell Library

the harsh climate and punishments meted out for my insubordination I grew stronger, taller and much more cynical.

After a period of time I became a valuable commodity. The Colony of New South Wales was devoid of all of England's little luxuries. If the Colony was to survive then it needed lots of labour to build homes, roads and bridges and, of most importance it required labourers to tend the livestock and grow crops. The only item the Colony was in fact not short of was convicts. The Colony was isolated from Mother England and unless it could support itself to some extent the residents could find themselves in dire straits.

I was eventually handed over to a settler, like a reward, to work long hours with no wage until I had seen out my seven years. I can't remember who I slaved for, and don't care. The only good to come out of this period of my life was that I tended horses. I was always good with horses. So I was no longer a seaboy, I was now a blacksmith. Horses trusted me, and I preferred their company to human beings. There was and is nothing in the world like a graceful grey filly.

Whilst I was learning my trade and biding my time until I received my ticket of leave, I began to take notice of my surroundings. As I have already told you, I was a good horseman and had seen the countryside of Kent. I could wax lyrical about the green rolling hills and the oak and elm trees, but I will not. Along with the climate, everything in New South Wales was different to my childhood experiences. The "bush" was stubborn; the indigenous people had never farmed it. Most of the colonists were scared of the Aborigines, with their own traditions and their own languages. I began to watch and learn. They could find water and food in this dry land, they could travel great distances without the aid of a compass and unlike my "betters" seemed to live a less complicated life. I began to learn their ways storing up my skills until I could put them into practise.

As time went by and Sydney town continued to grow, the land-hungry and curious pioneers began to explore more and more of the new land. There was hardly a week went by when even the convicts did not hear of a new animal or a new discovery. It seemed that everyone wanted to find the so-called inland sea or some such thing. After all, in those days there were no detailed maps of what turned out to be a continent. It seemed to me that if there was so much land just for the taking that on my release I could find myself a remote spot, take some horses and turn my back on the rest of society.

There were a few acquaintances that I made in my first few years in servitude. They may have thought that we were mates, but I kept my guard up, I did not let any of these coves know too much about me. The less they knew the less they could tell. These acquaintances were mostly from Ireland; in fact the whole colony was full of Irish convicts. I took up with Denis Hogan, Michael Finigan, Charles Neale and John McCarty alias John Kiddy alias John Davis.

What a good idea an alias was. I saw how John bamboozled the slow-witted authorities time and time again. He used his aliases to get himself out of many tight situations; this was something I decided to use if I ever found myself in a scrape again.

Some of my mates were hot-heads, Michael was a felon like me, and couldn't keep his mouth shut, he was fractious by nature and that landed him a charge of insubordination and a heavy punishment for his troubles. John McCarty was always light-fingered, that came from never having enough of anything, so what was left unattended he took. I only know of him being caught once, in Sydney, in 1826.

I was not a hothead like my Irish mates, I was ever the cool and calculating one, I knew how to keep my own council.

On 19 June 1833 I was given my Certificate of Freedom. At twenty-two years of age I was a grown man and I was never going to allow anyone to claim authority over me again. I was now my own master. Even if I could never leave the Colony, I was determined to quit Sydney and find my own space.

During my first few years in New South Wales overland expeditions had opened up the hinterland. Explorers, as these men were known, travelled in every conceivable direction. Hume and Hovell went south and reached the coast of Port Phillip in 1824, settlements were established at Portland and in 1835 John Batman landed at Port Phillip, whilst John Pascoe Fawkner established a further settlement on the banks of the Yarra River. Other parties penetrated the mountainous Gipps Land district in the 1840's. All these areas were remote, sparsely policed and naturally appealing to me, and my mates.

Port Phillip

I cannot remember the exact date that I arrived in the Port Phillip District, it is not important. With my freedom I could do what I pleased and travel where I chose, as long as I did not return to England. The area suited me. The population was small, about four and a half thousand people living in the town of Melbourne and almost seven hundred people in William's Town. There was far less cultivated land and a far smaller military and police force to contend with than in Sydney Town. I found the District of Port Phillip to my liking despite the presence of the Melbourne and County of Bourke Police Force, which had been formed in September 1836. By the time of my arrival in the vicinity Chief Constable William Wright commanded eleven constables and one scourger. As there were no real gaols in the District, the scourger was employed to flog minor offenders rather than imprisoning the poor sods.

The District of Port Phillip was remote, and hence a horse was considered to be of paramount importance to one's survival. All supplies were brought from Sydney or occasionally from the other penal settlement in Van Diemen's Land. Horses were the only form of transportation. A good horse was considered a status symbol to the "upper class" that infested Collins Street. I was a blacksmith so I could find my skills in demand but I did not wish to be at anyone's beck and call. Instead I teamed up with my old mates, Denis Hogan, Michael Finigan, Charles Neale and John McCarty.

Denis Hogan liked to believe that he was a born leader and to his credit he did dream up our horse stealing system. I didn't care if he fashioned himself as our leader. My intention was to keep my background and my unusual physical features out of the limelight. If anyone was going to be caught it was not going to be me.

Hogan's plan was simple. He and a few associates would keep a lookout for some good horseflesh. Once spotted the gang would check out the stabling arrangements of the horses and during the dead of night ride the horses away to our hideout. Once in our possession, the nags would be rested and their brands altered. The horses could then be sold on to anyone.

As I was blacksmith my job was to care for the horses and alter their brands. To do this I required stables, fodder, a plentiful water supply and space to exercise my charges. Our headquarters needed to be well away from Melbourne Town so that we did not attract the attention of the law, but also to be close enough to move horses back and forth with speed.

As you know I was literate, and so were a number of our gang, so when an advertisement appeared in the Port Phillip Herald in early 1841 regarding a new establishment called the Kinlochewe Inn, we took note. The advertisement announced that a new hotel on a large scale with every requisite to insure comfort had been opened at Kinlochewe, about eighteen miles from town. The advertisement suggested that the hotel

Kinlochewe Inn

would be perfect accommodation for all persons who had stations on the Sydney Road.[12]

I was well accustomed to travelling in the bush and so made my way to the Kinlochewe Inn to see if the establishment would suite as a base for our business operations. The area was perfect, and whilst not using the Inn itself we found that most of our requirements could be accommodated within close proximity of the Inn. We were officially in business in January 1841.

Initially our business prospered, the demand for high-quality horses rose as the population increased in the Port Phillip District. The gang was discreet at first, taking care not to purloin too many horses too often. Then Denis Hogan got cocky and came under the suspicion of the rudimentary police force. Hogan was captured and found guilty of horse stealing on the 26th April 1841. He was sentenced to fifteen years transportation.

---

12   Port Phillip Herald January 15, 1841

For the remainder of the gang there was no need to worry, Hogan kept his mouth shut and all we needed to do was postpone our business for a short while. Unfortunately not all of the gang had the brains to lie low. Charles Neale, who we called "The Doctor" decided to go it alone and was caught in the possession of Hugh Jamieson's mare in May 1841. "The Doctor" did not have a good alibi when found in the possession of the horse. He claimed that he had purchased the mare from Jamieson for half cash and the balance to be paid in three months. Of course Jamieson refuted this arrangement and "the Doctor" suffered the same fate as Hogan, fifteen years transportation.

In one of my rare articulate moments, I cautioned the remainder of the gang to be vigilant and to keep their sticky fingers to themselves, but they would not stay away from Melbourne, its pubs and its women. None of those things interested me. I was content to stay by the Merri Creek close to the Kinlochewe Inn, near Donnybrook.

My hackles were well and truly up on the 6th July 1841 when I read yet another large advertisement for the Kinlochewe Inn in the Port Phillip Herald. The Inn was to be let. A curse on Muirson for giving up his lease, he had turned a blind-eye to our business arrangements, it would be doubtful if a new lessee would take the same view. The Inn was described in such glowing terms by that pompous arse of an owner, he bragged that the Inn had ten well-finished spacious rooms, eight-stall stable, stockyards and replete in every other convenience. In glowing terms he added that the establishment came with one hundred and sixty-five acres of rich alluvial soil, ten acres of which was already under cultivation immediately behind the Inn with the holding extending to the Merri Creek[13]. Mr Sewell, Solicitor of Little Collins Street Melbourne, handled the leasing arrangement for the Inn. I had reason to hate this man in the future and

---

13   Port Phillip Herald July 6, 1841

could have saved myself a lot of grief if I had warned him off my patch sooner.

Despite the Inn's pending change of hands, the gang had run out of cash necessitating the resumption of our business dealings. Michael Finigan and his Irish mates showing no fear of the law went and snatched Captain Cole's nag. Cole made a real song and dance about the theft even going so far as to advertise a reward of five pounds, in the paper[14]. The horse was claimed to be valued at one hundred guineas. Along with the reward he gave a complete description of the beast, a dark brown horse, sixteen hands high, roman nose, long back, goose rumped, short tail, black points and branded CL under the mane.

What set this theft aside from many of the others was that Finigan had stolen the horse from its stable on the night of Monsieur Gautrot's Concert. So this effectively alerted the authorities in Port Phillip to the fact that the thieves were local lads and still active.

The Port Phillip Herald of course took up the hue and cry, and with its normal pomposity proclaimed:

> "Notwithstanding the recent and severe examples made of the gang of horse stealers, who infested Melbourne a few months since, by his Honour the Judge at the second criminal sittings of the Supreme Court, this serious crime, we regret to state, has not abated; indeed, the fellows go about the matter in a most barefaced manner…Verily Melbourne is getting a pretty name for murders, burglars, and other vagabonds".[15]

---

14   Port Phillip Herald August 18 1841
15   Port Phillip Herald July 30, 1841

The remnant of the gang then "acquired" a two-year old grey filly, which was branded L on the near shoulder, from Mr Logie. If I could have got my hands on the person who told Ex-Chief Constable William "Tulip" Wright where to look for the filly I would have killed him. Wright was keen to show that he still held the interests of the law-abiding community in high esteem, despite the fact that he was no longer the Chief Constable, and supplied Chief Constable Frederick Falkiner with all the details promptly.

Without any further hesitation Chief Constable Falkiner and Mr Logie apparently dashed off down the Sydney Road and conveniently took lodgings at the Kinlochewe Inn. Chief Constable Falkiner claimed that he was awakened by two men bringing the mail up from Melbourne to Sydney, the pompous braggart claimed that this was suspicious and he immediately knew something was in the wind. If it was so unusual and urgent, why did Logie and Falkiner stop for breakfast before taking chase, albeit that they did dine at 3.00am? By God I hope they suffered with indigestion!

After their fine breakfast Logie and Falkiner just happened to visit Mr Whitehead's station, which had only just been purchased by Mr Wood a former carter in Melbourne. Falkiner then claimed that someone told him, at this point of time, that I was living at the station, now isn't that just dandy? Of course they found the missing filly at the station. I had been set up. I had no notion of what was going on and as Michael Finigan and I strolled over to the paddock to feed the filly we saw two men saddling up the horse.

Chief Constable Falkiner introduced himself to Michael and me and asked us what we were doing. I tried to bluff him by saying that we were there to catch a black mare. Suddenly Falkiner turned his attention on me solely and demanded my name. I gave my name as Smith, and Falkiner said: "Just the very person I wanted".

I was in big trouble, so I bolted, being young and fit I thought I could outrun him. I made off toward the Plenty River, and thought that I would lose my assailant in the bush. Falkiner mounted his nag and caught up with me in the river. I would have got away if the bugger hadn't struck me with the butt of his whip and knocked me unconscious. The next thing I knew was that I had been handcuffed and tied to Falkiner on his horse.

Only on reaching Melbourne did the coward Mr Logie swear that the filly found at Mr Whitehead's station was his property. Then up chimed Constable Boyle and John Stewart swearing in unison that they had seen me riding the filly on Tuesday. I was immediately remanded and placed in the stockade.

The Port Phillip Herald had me convicted before my trial. How could I receive a fair trial when they printed the following piffle?

> "The prisoner does not deny being acquainted with Hogan, who was transported at the late criminal court for a similar offence, and there can be little doubt that he is also one of that daring band, who have stolen Captain Cole's and other persons horses within the last few weeks. Mr Wright's activity in acquiring, and his promptitude in communicating the minutest particulars are well deserving the utmost praise, and too much credit cannot be given to Mr Falkiner for the manner in which he discharges his duties as Chief Constable, the present being a very good example of his efficiency".[16]

---

16   Port Phillip Herald August 13, 1841

So I was banged up in Melbourne's temporary gaol. Well I could handle it. I'd been in enough gaols before. Then the fun and games began. Firstly I was being referred to as Thomas Tookey, illiterate fools couldn't even spell my surname. So I decided not to correct them hoping that the authorities would not connect me with my past if they were unaware of my real name.

Blessed with an exceptional memory I can recall that on the 17th August, 1841 I was committed to stand trial for horse stealing in the Supreme Court at Melbourne. I was remanded, until the next session due to the absence of a material witness named Betts, who had not been served with a subpoena. In fact none of the witnesses had been served with subpoenas. I never heard of the fella Betts. I reckon that the prosecution was buying time because there was no real evidence to convict me.

I can still hear His Honour Judge John Walpole Willis in his lardy-dah voice remarking that it was very extraordinary that "so many witnesses were absent". The Judge concluded by saying, that "horse stealing is too good a trade. It carries on to such an extent that it is dangerous to have a horse tethered by your own house, the money received by the nefarious practice enables parties accused to defeat the ends of justice". Judge Willis knew what he was talking about, I had often advised persons not to give testimony against me, and if they were amenable even slipped a few coppers their way.

On the following Tuesday, by special appointment I was again brought before Judge Willis, and naturally the dim-witted prosecutor had still not given notice to the witnesses, my trial was again adjourned.

My next appearance in court was on Friday the 26th August 1841, by then I was getting pretty familiar with the carryings on at the Supreme Court and with Judge John Walpole Willis. Judge Willis it appeared knew his law, but was noted for his many disagreements with his colleagues. Willis came to hear my case on the re-bound, he had been educated at Cambridge and was initially appointed a puisne judge on the King's Bench in Upper Canada in 1827. In the following year he had a falling out with the Attorney General, and was eventually removed from his position by Lieutenant Governor, Sir Peregrine Maitland. As Willis' conduct was treated as an error of judgment he was appointed a judge in Demerara, British Giuana. He returned to England in 1836 and was finally made a judge of the Supreme Court of New South Wales, arriving in Sydney in 1837. By 1839 Willis had quarrelled with Chief Justice Dowling and therefore Governor Sir George Gipps arranged for Willis to be appointed resident judge in Melbourne.[17]

My trial commenced and a jury was empanelled before Mr James Croke (pity he didn't croak) made a further application to postpone the trial, as he had yet again, been unable to procure the presence of important witnesses in the case.

Judge Willis, by then, was in no mood to be trifled with but Croke rambled on about how he had made every exertion to obtain the appearance of the witnesses and then he stated that he was ready to swear an affidavit to his diligence in the matter. Croke then prattled on with a pretty little speech to the effect of "as the heinousness, and importance of the crime, of so very frequent occurrence of late, imperatively called for investigation, he hoped his Honour would afford him an opportunity of bringing the case before the court which at present he was utterly unable to do".[18]

---

17 Dictionary of Australian Biography.
18 Port Phillip Herald August 31, 1841

Redmond Barry

My Counsel, Mr Redmond Barry, opposed the application on the grounds that this was the second time the case had been postponed, and stated that it would be harsh on me to be retained in gaol.

His Honour had no time for me, his reasons for granting the further postponement being that as my case was of considerable magnitude and great importance to the public, he thought himself justified and as Mr Croke was willing to support his application by affidavit, my case was postponed until the 15th September 1841.

So I languished in Melbourne's gaol, but I made my incarceration as difficult as I could for my gaolers. They were in living fear of me. They knew I had friends and they knew that if I was freed I could and would carry out retributions on them and their families.

My trial finally took place on Wednesday the 15th September 1841 before Residing Judge Willis. A jury was empanelled. I will list the name of the jurors and their occupations, for many of them considered that they were my betters, but the majority were common tradesmen and innkeepers:

Alexander Broadfoot, of Craig & Broadfoot, Queen Street, Melbourne;

W. Coulson, of the Melbourne Hotel, Flinders Street, Melbourne;

John Cummins, builder of Flinders Street, Melbourne;

Francis James Cox, baker and grocer of Little Flinders Street, Melbourne;

A. Crockett, of Crocket & Willoughby General Stores, Elizabeth and Little Flinders Street Melbourne;

John Bullivant, of the Waterloo Tavern, Little Collins Street, Melbourne;

Ebenezer Brown, coachbuilder and wheelwright of Lonsdale Street, Melbourne;

John Brown, compositor of Little Collins Street Melbourne;

Henry Baker, innkeeper of the Imperial Inn, Collins Street, Melbourne;

George Buckingham, general agent of Collins Street, Melbourne;

Charles Beswick, of Charles & James wholesale and retail dealers, Collins Street, Melbourne[19];

and finally Sylvester John Browne (whose son would later profit by my escapades), landholder of a 313-acre estate he named "Hartlands" situated in the valley of Heidelberg. Browne also owned numerous properties in and around Melbourne, including some Melbourne blocks, 70 acres at Toorak near the present site of Government House and 2,000 acres situated on the Darebin near Northcote.[20]

I was placed at the bar and indicted with stealing a grey mare, the property of William Logie. A second count in the indictment also laid the mare as the property of James Robinson Uneet, a settler of Annikie Yeo-Yang.[21] Oh, they were out to get me no matter what. The authorities were going to make this charge stick.

---

19 Kerr's Melbourne Almanac 1841 & 1842.
20 Heidelberg – The Land and Its People 1838-1900 – Donald S Garden: Melbourne University Press 1972.
21 Kerr's Melbourne Almanac 1841 & 1842

Mr Croke, the Crown Prosecutor, proceeded to state the case and ranted and raved about the enormity of the crime of horse stealing, its' frequent commission and the necessity for the suppression of the crime. Mr Croke then called on the Jury even "to stretch their consciences a little"[22].

The Judge interrupted Mr Croke and feeling rather pleased with his speech Croke obliged and sat down.

Mr Barry, my Counsel, commenced his address by saying that he was astonished to hear the Crown Prosecutor call on the jury to "stretch their consciences" to convict a fellow creature! Mr Barry was so indignant that he commented that such an address was never made to a British Jury since the days of Judge Jeffries, 'the hanging judge'.

My defence was basic, namely there were discrepancies in the evidence and several connecting links in the chain of evidence were deficient. Mr Barry concluded by saying to the Jury that there was no evidence of the taking and carrying away of the animal.

It was a sterling effort by Mr Barry, but I was a goner, especially after the Judge charged the Jury as follows:

> "Gentlemen of the Jury, you have heard with attention the lengthy evidence which has been adduced, and I am glad to see that some of you have been taking notes. I must first turn my attention to the point of law mooted by Mr Barry, with regard to the animo furandi of the case. The prisoner was seen to go to the station of Messrs. Watson and Hunter, and to take a mare from thence; and although the witness Betts cannot identify the mare, still the proof of her having a white blaze on her face will be a subject for your consideration. We find by the evidence of Stewart the fact of her having been taken away, and

---

22   Port Phillip Herald September 15, 1841

being in the possession of the prisoner. Mr Logie also went in search of her; from private information he found the mare under circumstances which you must judge of, and although the prisoner stated to Stewart that he did not own the mare, still evidence sufficient has been adduced of his riding and being in possession of her. Gentlemen, I trust you will do your duty, but not imitating Jeffries, who, although a very great man, was still a bad one in my opinion. Mr Barry alluded to a reward that was held out to witnesses by the Legislature for the conviction of parties guilty of cattle stealing, those acts are, however, not now in force, they have ceased to exist. I must congratulate the community on the praiseworthy institution which has been formed among them, and from which the most beneficial results are to be expected. An institution formed for the suppression of crime, based on the laws of the great Alfred, that which oblige the hundreds to make good the injuries committed on the few. Such associations are extremely worthy, I must say, of imitation; they establish the best possible kind of police. It will, I trust, deter those, already habituated to crime, who have before been exiled from their homes for their mal-practices (which applies to the prisoner) from the further commission of such actions, and teach them that honesty in the end is always the best policy. Encouraged by these cheering prospects, I shall proceed gladly in the execution of my arduous duties, invigorated in mind by the brightening horizon of morality around me. It goes beyond this world gentlemen, it affects the next, by preventing deluded beings from committing crimes for which they should not only have to answer for in this world, but in another. I trust, gentlemen, that on the evidence alone, you will rest your verdict; that the character of the prisoner, or the heinousness of his crime, will not affect your verdict; those, gentlemen, are subjects for my after consideration, and mine alone – they will weigh with me as to the sentence I shall pass upon the prisoner if he is found guilty.

I now leave the case in your hands, satisfied that you will do it that justice it merits, and weigh the evidence that has been adduced with an impartial mind".[23]

I bet you will not be surprised to hear that the Jury did not even leave the box, after an extremely short deliberation they found me guilty. His Honour Judge Willis then sentenced me to transportation for fifteen years.

Michael Finigan was also found guilty of horse stealing on that same day, but the newspapers didn't show any interest in his trial.

So I was to be transported again. Whilst awaiting my relocation I was housed in the gaol, in Collins Street West. The gaol was a brick structure with shingle roof, divided into three compartments, and having two small cells for solitary confinement. The gaol was a rough and ready building, but it did not have a stockade.[24] I was not going to behave for my gaolers, why should I? My freedom had been taken and hence I was aggressive threatening all those within earshot. The townsfolk supplied my only source of entertainment during the period of my incarceration. I was housed close by the site of the new Melbourne Gaol, an isolated spot. The Government had brought in building materials that were left unguarded at night. Building supplies were in very short demand, and so each night law-abiding residents of Melbourne visited the site and purloined materials. I never saw the completion of the new gaol. So much for my "betters"!

---

23 Port Phillip Herald September 17,1841
24 The Old Melbourne Gaol 1841 – National Trust of Australia.

Port Arthur

I was supposed to be imprisoned at Cockatoo Island in New South Wales, but instead I was transported to Port Arthur in Van Diemen's Land on the steam ship "The Sea Horse". Even I could not escape the industrial revolution, which dramatically altered the world I had been born into. The Sea Horse was only the third steam ship to visit Port Phillip, so my journey to my next place of incarceration was quicker and safer than any other journey by sea that I had heard of or experienced.

I arrived in Van Diemen's Land on the 16th February 1843, the time when the colony was accepting its largest quota of convicts. The year before my arrival the intake of convicts peaked at five thousand, three hundred and twenty-nine. The convict population exceeded thirty thousand by the middle of the decade, and represented forty-seven percent of the Island's population.[25]

Port Arthur, in Van Diemen's Land was one of the few secondary punishment stations operating in the colonies. By the time of my arrival at Port Arthur, convicts were employed in ship building, shoemaking, smithing, timber and brick-making, nothing new to me, I had seen this

---

25   www.tourtasmania.com/tasfaq/history/convict.html

all at Carter's Barracks. A large flourmill and granary were in the process of being erected at this time, this would also provide more backbreaking work for the likes of me.

Convicts were forced to labour in silence at Port Arthur. For many felons it was a most depressing and soul-destroying establishment. I had heard the stories of past prisoners such as the like of Minnehan, who battered another prisoner to death whilst returning from a stone-breaking expedition on a chain gang. Minnehan, was sentenced to be hanged and his body anatomised and dissected, the poor sod was credited with saying that he was sick of living and "Thanks be to God, you cannot dissect my soul, although you can my body".[26]

The pompous and arrogant guards wasted no time in telling me and the other "new hands", that we would never escape the gaol. This was tantamount to issuing me with a challenge and I immediately set about examining my new surrounds and planning my escape from this cesspit and its inhabitants.

There is a narrow strip of land, which is called Eaglehawk Neck, which separates the Tasman Peninsula and the penal settlement. This piece of land was the obvious escape route for convicts and so there was an officer, a sergeant and twenty-five soldiers stationed at the Neck complete with officers' quarters, military barracks, store and jetty. A semaphore station provided for communications with the rest of the peninsula. The station was used principally to send information regarding absconders from Port Arthur to authorities on the Peninsula and in Hobart Town. To further dissuade felons to attempt escape via the Neck, there was also the infamous "Dogline". Guard dogs were tethered at short intervals across

---

26   Timeline of Van Dieman's Land www.labyrinth.net.au/~saul/history/tasmania.html

the Neck to guard against escaping convicts, the dogs were supposed to be an impassable barrier. Melville described the guard dogs as:

> "Those out of the way pretenders to dogship were actually rationed and borne on the government's books, and rejoiced in such sobriquets as Caesar, Pompey, Ajax, Achilles, Ugly Mug, Jowler, Tear'em and Muzzle'eme. There were black, the white, the brindle, the grey and the grisly, the rough and the smooth, the crop-eared and the lop-eared, the gaunt and the grim. Every four-footed, black-fanged individual among them would have taken first prize in his own class of ugliness and ferocity at any show".[27]

Convict handlers were responsible for the guard dogs' care. The handlers feed the dogs and cared for the canines in every possibly way. If I had remained in that God-forsaken place, I would have volunteered my service as a dog handler. I've told you before, that I held dogs and horses is far greater esteem than any human being.

The guards at Port Arthur also relished telling us poor sods about the shark infested waters around the Neck and recounted bloodthirsty tales of the outcome of anybody that attempted to swim to freedom. I had my doubts about all these tales, especially as I had heard all about the successful escape from Port Arthur by the famous bushranger Martin Cash, barely a year before I arrived at the settlement. Cash, Lawrence Kavanagh and George Jones escaped Port Arthur and on reaching the Neck undressed and tied their clothes in bundles on their heads and entered the water. All three men made it across to dry land but lost their clothes in the crossing. They stole clothes and provisions from a road-gang hut and survived at large for several months. They were eventually

---

27   Melville, c, 1840 – Guide to Historical Places – Eaglehawk Neck – History – www.parks.tas.gov.au

re-captured and Cash and Kavanagh were transported to Norfolk Island and Jones was hanged in May 1844.[28]

I was by my thirty-second year what you might call a hardened felon. Nothing that the cruel and savage guards could mete out in the way of punishment would break my spirit, although on occasions they nearly broke my body.

I made my first unsuccessful bid for freedom on the 16th March 1843, exactly one month after my arrival. For my efforts I received one hundred straps from the Cat-O-Nine Tails. I had recovered sufficiently by the 3rd April 1843 to be found guilty of misconduct and therefore placed in solitary confinement for seven days. Weakened by this treatment I needed time to recover, but again found myself charged with yet another misdemeanour, that of disobeying orders, and received for my troubles a further five days in solitary confinement. On the 22nd September 1843 I was found guilty of idleness and was sent to labour in chains. On the 4th December 1843 I was again found guilty of misconduct, this time for being absent from my gang without leave and surprise, surprise I received yet a further three days in solitary confinement. The new year had hardly started, in fact it was the 6th January 1844, when I was again found guilty of misconduct and was also suspected of stealing apples. Of course I bloody well stole apples! On the paltry rations I received and the various forms of punishments handed out to my I was starving, if I hadn't stolen food I could have died of hunger!

On the 24th January 1844, I was still smarting over my most recent punishment when I was yet once more found guilty of misconduct and given a further seven days solitary confinement. I tell you with my

---

28 Guide to Historical Places – Eaglehawk Neck - www.parks.tas.gov.au

reputation I only had to look at a poxy guard twice and I was up on a charge.²⁹

So much solitary confinement had given me plenty of time to plan and more determination than ever to escape. The months of hard labour had made me physically strong. On the 28th August 1844 I finally escaped from the penal settlement at Port Arthur.

As an escaped convict, my first priorities were to ditch my convict clobber and to put as many miles between me, and the hell-hole, Port Arthur. It was difficult to acquire clothing seeing as almost half of the population of Van Diemen's Island were convicts, and the other half were so terrified of convicts and aborigines that they were well armed and very suspicious of unfamiliar faces.

Speaking of faces, mine was very distinct and well documented by the authorities. My official description at the time of my escape was:

Trade: Blacksmith	Height: Five feet six inches
Age: Thirty	Complexion: Swarthy
Head: Oval	Hair: Dark brown
Visage: Oval	Forehead: Retreating
Eyebrows: Dark brown	Eyes: Dark brown
Nose: Large	Mouth: Large
Chin: Dimpled	

In the authorities pedantic manner my "irregularities" were also meticulously noted and included as: scar on right eyebrow, mole on left side of neck, scars on the upper part of neck from an instrument, five dots on my left hand between thumb and finger, ST tattooed on my left

---

29 Toke's indent (Con 16/1) Archives of Tasmania.

arm, scar on my left hand, a man and woman tattooed inside my right arm and of course I still had "an impediment in speech".[30]

So what do you expect? I had had a few scrapes and my tattoos were done in times of boredom and proved I could endure any sort of pain. However my distinguished looks made me easily recognisable and if the bastards decided to offer a reward for my capture, I would be fair game for anyone that spotted me. I have already told you about Martin Cash and his escape from Port Arthur, the reward offered for him must have sorely tempted the whole population:

> REWARD
> FIFTY GOLD SOVEREIGNS AND A CONDITIONAL PARDON
> Whereas the three convicts [Runaways from Port Arthur] MARTIN CASH, GEORGE JONES, AND LAWRENCE KAVENHAGH,
> Whose descriptions are as under, stand charged with having committed divers, Capital Felonies, and are now illegally at large.
> This is to give Notice that I am authorised by His Excellency the Lieutenant-Governor to offer a Reward of Fifty Sovereigns to any person or persons who shall apprehend or cause to be apprehended and lodged in safe custody either of the said Felons; and should this service be performed by a Convict, then in addition to such pecuniary Reward a CONDITIONAL PARDON[31]

I was never anyone's fool and knew that it was no point in heading for Hobart Town as I would be easily recognised by the military and ex-convicts and would have found my way back into gaol before I could stammer my name.

---

30 Toke's indent(Con 16/1) Archives of Tasmania.
31 John Doxey's Australia – http://pages.zdnet.com/jojogunne/australia/id7.html.

Port Arthur

So I headed to the midland area of Van Diemen's Land, hoping to find some quiet location where I would not arouse any suspicion. I found myself in the vicinity of Oatlands within fourteen days of my escape.

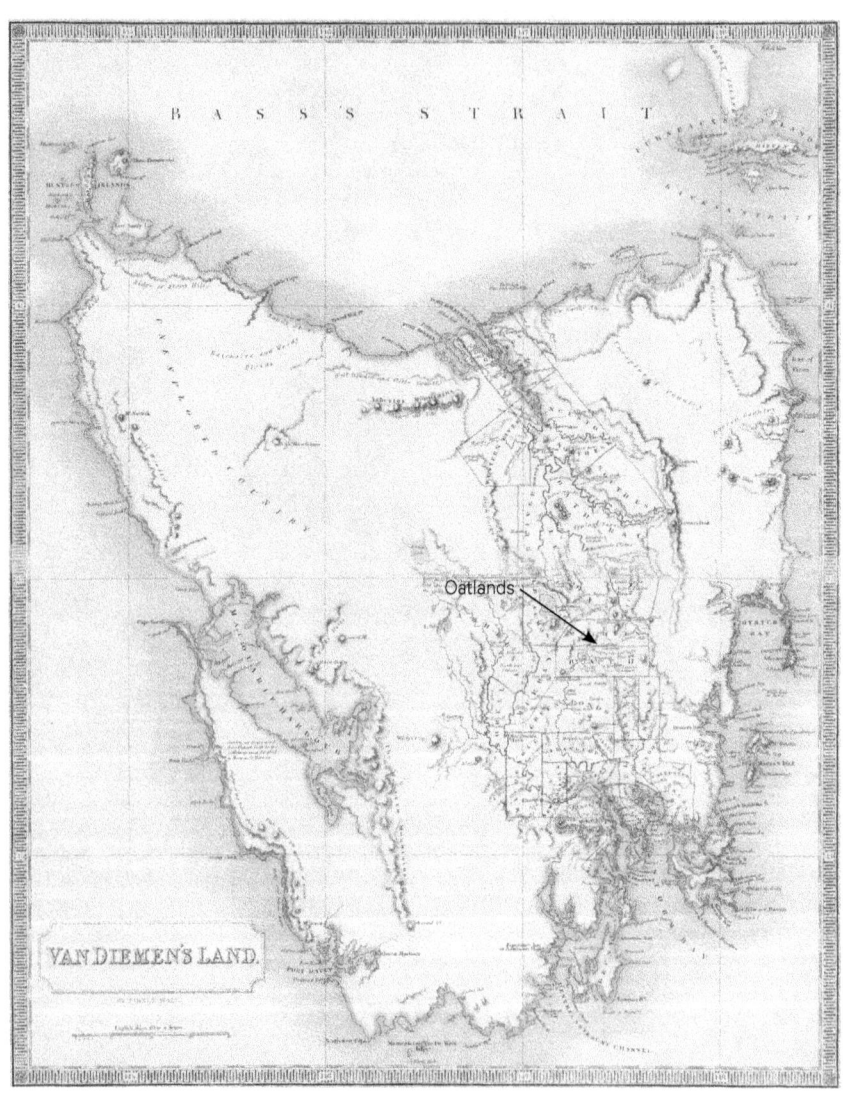

Van Diemen's Land map. Courtesy of Tasmanian Archive and Heritage Office Commons

OATLANDS

You probably haven't even heard of Oatlands have you? Well let me tell you in 1844 it was quite some town. Governor Lachlan Macquarie of New South Wales was credited as founding the town in 1811. Macquarie was travelling north from Hobart Town in 1811 when he is said to have passed through a beautiful valley covered with honeysuckle and flowering gums. Ten years later on Sunday the 3rd June 1821 at 12.15pm. Macquarie named the town and wrote in his journal "This is a very eligible situation for a town, being well watered and in the midst of rich fertile country"[32]. He named the town after the original Oatlands, which is situated in Surrey England, and where King George III kept his stud of merino sheep.

Macquarie had a real liking for the area and even suggested that all the buildings erected in the town should be constructed out of stone or brick. However, Oatlands did not show much progress for some time, the regular stopping place on the north-south route, between Hobart and Launceston remained Macquarie Springs.[33]

---

32   A History of Lower Midlands by J.S.Weeding
33   A History of Lower Midlands by J.S.Weeding.

So I chose Oatlands, seventy-three miles from Launceston, and fifty-two miles from Hobart as my base. I thought that it was a bit of a backwater but unfortunately the town was well serviced with an established military garrison, a Court House and a gaol. How was I to know all that?

My first and only interest at this time of my life on the run was to become self-sufficient. To achieve self-sufficiency, I needed to obtain supplies, money and a gun. I had no qualms as to how or whom I took these items from. I had been stripped of all my worldly possession when I was transported to New South Wales, so it wouldn't hurt if some wealthy settler was divested of a few paltry goods in return.

I had been on the run for some weeks and no one had reported anything taken by me, so I felt lucky. On the 10th September 1844, I entered a nice little dwelling and had just commenced to look around when Mr Robinson disturbed me. Such a coward he was. I simply pointed the gun I had acquired at him, he stood there trembling and I calmly picked up a few essential items and left. Robinson must have taken himself straight off to the authorities and reported my visit. Mr M.A.Dore, also reported me when I paid him a visit on the 15th September 1844. The snivelling little "gentlemen" claimed that I had not only stolen their goods but that I had put them in "bodily fear".[34]

September was turning out to be a bad month for me, I had been tried in September 1841 in the District of Port Phillip and in September 1844 I was again captured and placed in custody in Oatlands. Lucky for me there are few surviving records pertaining to my time in Van Diemen's Land. Even the record of my trial for "stealing from the person of, and putting in fear, James Cuthbertson Sutherland, twenty pounds of flour valued at one shilling and other articles of his property, has not survived.

---

34   Toke's indent (Con 16/1) Archives of Tasmania.

I can tell you however, that the events leading up to the trial were a bit of a farce.

I was to be tried at the Tenth Session of the Oatlands Supreme Court on the 3rd October 1844. It had rained heavily for some days leading up to this my first appearance in the Supreme Court of Tasmania. As a consequence the nearby Lake Crescent broke its banks and flooded the surrounding low-lying area. Rather than simply stating the obvious, that the day's proceeding had been postponed due to flooding, The Hobart Town Courier and Van Diemen's Land Gazette reported the event as follows:

> Wednesday being the day appointed for the opening of the Midland Sessions, in due time a goodly throng of prosecutors, witnesses, and jurors, with the various officers of the Court, exclusive of the Judge, assembled at the threshold of the Court awaiting the usual announcement of its opening by the appointed officer. Hour succeeded hour, however, and the ... official adverted to still continued mute, until at length it began to be whispered about that His Honour Mr Justice Montagu had been unable to accomplish his journey in the present broken state of the roads, and that the business of the Session was in consequence adjourned until the following day[35]

On the 4th October 1844 His Honour Mr Justice Montagu entered the Court punctually at ten o'clock, and the prisoners (fifteen in number) were duly arraigned and disposed of. The first prisoner to be brought before Mr Justice Montagu was Phillip Hughes, a soldier of the 96th regiment, belonging to the detachment at Ross. Hughes was charged with a burglary in the dwelling house of Mr. Robert Sutton, a storekeeper. Upon the suggestion of the Judge, the Attorney-General abandoned the

---

35   The Hobart Town, Courier and Van Diemen's Land Gazette, Tuesday October 8, 1844.

case of burglary, upon the grounds that the building in which the offence (stealing a gun) was committed was not a dwelling-house in the legal sense of the term. Hughes was convicted of the larceny only, and being his first offence "the Judge sentenced him, with much kind advice and good feeling, to six months imprisonment only in the common gaol. It appeared the prisoner had fallen from a general course of honesty under the common instigation of intoxication"[36].

The real hilarity, for those present that day, with the exception of the prisoners of course, was the case of Thomas Fitzgerald and John Frury who were indicted for assaulting and robbing James Mount-stephens' of a watch, in the streets of Bothwell, on one evening in September. The prisoners had previously been seen in the public house together by the prosecutor (an officer of the police). The prosecutor arrested the prisoners at their respective places of residence, within half an hour after commission of the offence. A raw recruit of the 51st Regiment, stated that he was "standing at ease" (in other words relieving himself) beneath the window of the house where the prisoners had proceeded after the commission of the offence, stated that he heard the prisoners talking over the exploit and saying they had 'planted' the watch where nobody would find it. The simplicity of this witness, "who delivered his information with all the solemn pretension of the goose-step,"[37] afforded some merriment to the Court. The defence turned chiefly upon the prosecutor having drank three glasses of ale and played a game of bagatelle at the public-house prior to the robbery. This did not appear to the jury to bear any significance upon the after part of the evening's proceedings. In spite of the window revelation by the recruit, the watch was discovered by means of an anonymous letter written to the real owner Adam Moran, from who it appeared Mount-stephen had borrowed it to teach him how to

---

36   The Hobart Town, Courier and Van Diemen's Land Gazette, Tuesday October 8, 1844.
37   The Hobart Town, Courier and Van Diemen's Land Gazette, Tuesday October 8, 1844.

tell the time of day. This letter, which was couched in very mysterious terms, advised Moran to search beneath a side line post of a certain town allotment, where he would discover his time-piece in a piece of rag. Moran was not to forget to deposit a pound note in the watch's place to reward his friendly correspondent for his trouble. Moran disinterred the watch without depositing the proposed gratuity in its place. The learned Judge, in his charge to the jury, pointed to some confusion in the evidence, resulting apparently from the stupidity of the recruit, and thus the prisoners received the benefit in their acquittal. In calling the jury's attention to discrepancies, His Honour complimented the constabulary upon their integrity as witnesses. I knew then and there that this Judge would always take the side of the constabulary and I was done for.

By the time of the conclusion of the second case, one of the jurors had nodded off to sleep. The juror's cigar dropped from his hand and set the jury box alight. There was a great hue and cry about this. The wits in the courtroom joked about all that water outside and a fire inside. Very funny, their lives were not on trial. Once the jury box was secured, and the Judge had called the court to order the proceedings continued.

Eventually I was placed in the dock, and charged with stealing from the person of and putting in fear James Cuthbertson Sutherland, twenty pounds of flour, valued at one shilling and other articles of his property. No mention was made about the thefts from Messrs Robinson and Dore.

Once again I was referred to as Thomas Tookey, but for the first time I was also described as a bushranger. A bushranger was simply then, an escaped convict living in the bush, a definition that suited me fine. I found out later in life that it was very prestigious to be called a bushranger.

I pleaded guilty to the indictment. "The impression was that the offence was one of the mildest character committed by this prisoner and his associates, and that he did wisely in acknowledging himself guilty of a lesser crime rather than be convicted of a greater".[38]

Sentence of death was recorded against me, with the usual intimation, by the Judge, that my life would be spared.

My first death sentence but I knew the sentence would not be carried out. So many other offenders had been convicted of far more heinous a crime and all that had befallen their fate was yet another stint in gaol in yet another penal colony.

Mr Justice Montagu did lodge a recommendation with the Colonial Secretary that mercy should be extended to me on condition that I was transported for life beyond the sea. In typical public service fashion the Colonial Secretary recorded my sentence of death and recommended that my life be spared on the condition that I underwent some secondary punishment.[39] I suppose this should have been a relief, but for such a small crime, I was yet again to be transported to yet another of His Majesty's hellholes.

The Lieutenant Governor, Sir John Eardley-Wilmot, considered the Executive Council and the Puisne Judge's Reports of my case and decided to extend Mercy to me on the condition that I was transported for life beyond the sea. I was to be sent to Norfolk Island.[40]

---

38 The Hobart Town Courier and Van Diemen's Land Gazette, Tuesday October 8, 1844.
39 Secretary's Minutes of 1 November 1844 No.L2418.
40 Secretary's Minutes of 1 November 1844 No L2418.

Norfolk Island

On the 6th March 1788, the British flag was raised on Norfolk Island. This was just six weeks after the First Fleet arrived at Botany Bay to establish the penal colony of New South Wales. Lieutenant Phillip Gidley King, seven freemen and fifteen convicts became the first occupants of Norfolk Island. Their occupation was to make available masts and sails from pine and flax for the refurbishment of British ships and to prevent the island falling into the ownership of the French.[41]

Norfolk Island became the dumping ground for New South Wales' worst felons. These lost souls were used as free labour to produce food for Sydney.

I had arrived in Sydney, as a callow youth in 1828, and by then Norfolk Island was infamous and often referred to as the 'Hell of the Pacific'. Due to the island's inaccessibility Sir Thomas Brisbane, Governor of New South Wales, had decided that Norfolk Island was an ideal place to send the most recalcitrant convicts "forever to be excluded from all hope of return"[42].

---

41   Norfolk Island – The First Settlement. www.pitcairners.org/settlements.html
42   Norfolk Island – The First Settlement www.pitcairners.org/settlements.html

All convicts in New South Wales were familiar with the stories of Norfolk Island and its gaol. Many convicts were sentenced to remain in heavy chains for the term of their natural lives. Most convicts were chained as they worked from sunrise to sunset. We had all heard about the convict, in a field gang, who had raised his hoe and split the head of the convict in front of him. His action was not one of malice or revenge, but because he knew that his punishment would be death, and death would be his only release from the horrendous life he lived.[43]

Punishments at Norfolk Island included hard labour, lashings, dumb-cells (which excluded light and sound), solitary confinement, increased workloads and decreased rations.

In 1845 I joined the swelling ranks of convicts, there were in fact one thousand two hundred of us miscreants on the Island. Major Childs had just become the Commandant and had received strict instructions from the New South Wales Government that twice-convicted men (such as the likes of me) were to adhere to regulations including:

1. Each convict must perform compulsory labour not for himself but for the Government. Compulsory and unrequited toil must be the rule and steadfastly adhered to.
2. No marks for good behaviour or good work, no private gardens where a man might work for himself.
3. The lash was to be reinstated, and used.[44]

Informers were encouraged and poor sods like me were often brought before the Magistrates' Court for minor breaches even if our actions were unintentional. As a Protestant, I was in the minority. The majority

---

43 Norfolk Island – the Second Settlement wwwpitcainers.org/settlements.html
44 Childs and The Mutiny – http://homepages.paradise.net.nz/r-c/mutiny.html

of prisoners were Irish Catholics and great believers they were too. None of us faired better and even the Ministers of religion were encouraged to report on their church members misdemeanours.

On the 15th July 1845 I was sentenced to ten days solitary confinement for absconding. This was an experience I have never forgotten. I was imprisoned in a dark underground cell and like all other convicts on the Island I grew to dread this punishment more than the lash. Many men lost their minds in solitary confinement, which could last for a period of up to ninety days. I had extreme powers of endurance, but even I did not know how long I could remain sane in a solitary confinement cell.

I was thirty-four years old and accustomed to backbreaking physical toil. The lash and poor rations only fuelled my determination to survive. My resentment of authority in any shape or form became harder and I thrived on my hatred for the government, its legal system and its sycophantic followers.

I had a natural distrust of my convict brethren, and took pride in my reputation as a violent and serious felon. To enhance my reputation I threatening and occasionally assaulted fellow convicts. Eventually my behaviour was reported to the authorities and on the 25th August 1845 I was charged and found guilty of assault. I was sentenced to eighteen months hard labour.

My sentence of hard labour at that Hell of the Pacific saw me placed in heavy irons, and sent to work all day, no matter the weather, in the stone quarry or the lime shed. This backbreaking work left me in such a state of exhaustion, that I was not able to take part in the infamous mutiny in June 1846.

The mutiny was triggered by Magistrate Barrow issuing yet another of his unjust orders. Let me digress here for a moment whilst I tell you about Samuel Barrow. Barrow's used every bit of guile he had in his evil little brain to swell the record of crimes alleged to have been committed by inmates of the gaol at Norfolk Island. He also created new crimes and selected men of the worst character to become constables on the Island. The constables were employed to provoke convicts to commit crimes. Some of the men Barrow's enlisted from Hobart Town, who often were tickets-of-leave, were permitted to antagonise superior officers who did not agree with Barrow. "..in 11 months he attended no religious services... He sent prisoners in chains to work on Saturday afternoons free time as part of punishment and one time an overseer was murdered".[45]

To anger and incite the inmates further Barrow ordered all the overseers to remove all cooking pots and kettles from the convicts. The pots and kettles were made by the convicts and used to prepare our uncooked food after the weighing and issuing of the rations by the cooks. Barrow with Major Child's consent, decided that this custom was to cease and that all food in the future would be cooked and served in the cookhouse.

After lock-up one evening the kettles, pots and pannikins were removed and placed in the Island's locker-room. When the inmates found out what had happened some convicts broke open the locker-room and retrieved the pots and pans. During breakfast a convict called William Westwood shouted, "Follow me! We will kill all..." he seized a hatchet and with twelve others, who armed themselves with hoes and spades killed an overseer and several guards.

The mutiny was over in less than half an hour, however every man with blood on his clothes was seized. Fifty-two men were ironed, and

---

45   Childs and The Mutiny – http://homepages.paradise.net.nz/r-c/mutiny.html.

twenty-six committed for trial. On the 23rd September a judge from Van Diemen's Land sentenced twelve convicts to be hanged, including William Westwood.[46] Westwood, or Jacky Jacky as he was known, was eventually hanged on the 13th October, 1846 he was twenty-seven years old.

I knew nothing of Westwood and his associates trials until after the fact, as only the day before, on the 22nd September 1845 I had yet again received a further fourteen days solitary confinement.

By the late 1840's the cost of maintaining Norfolk Island as a penal settlement was becoming prohibitive, and Port Arthur became much more attractive to the authorities if only because it was less costly to run. Visitors to the Island also began to speak out about our treatment. The Catholic Bishop of Hobart, Dr Robert Wilson, was one such person; he wrote, I believe, a damming report about the number of prisoners that were routinely flogged. Not that this did me much good as between the 16th April 1847 and the 23rd February 1848 I was consigned to continual hard labour having been convicted on five occasions of petty offences.

Unbeknown to me and the other inmates of Norfolk Island, there was also a move by Earl Grey, in the British Parliament, to give the Island to the inhabitants of Pitcairn Island. I expect you have never heard of the Pitcairn Islanders; they were the descendants of the mutiny of the "Bounty" and their Tahitian-Polynesian wives. I even wonder if you remember that Bligh was the Captain of the Bounty. Bligh was the fourth Governor of New South Wales and was embroiled in yet another rebellion, the Rum Rebellion, and was effectively imprisoned from 1808 to 1810 in New South Wales.

---

[46] Childs and The Mutiny – http://homepages.paradise.net.nz/r-c/mutiny.html.

In 1787, William Bligh took command of the "Bounty" and sailed to Tahiti to obtain a cargo of breadfruit. Captain Bligh was said to be a keen disciplinarian and favoured flogging as a punishment, he was also said to cut rations and to work his men so hard that even his first mate Fletcher Christian found it impossible to agree with him. In Tahiti some of the crew of the "Bounty" became involved with Tahitian women, when it was time to leave Tahiti the crew mutinied. Bligh and his supporters were set adrift in a launch and after a forty-one day voyage succeeded in reaching Timor.

Fletcher Christian, with eight mutineers and eighteen Tahitians occupied Pitcairn Island and made it their home. The Pitcairn community was not discovered by the outside world until 1808. Due to England's preoccupation with the Napoleonic War the news of the outcome of the mutineers' fate was not further investigated until 1814. By 1825 the Pitcairners were outgrowing the resources of the island and had sent word to the British Government that they would like to be re-located.

So the British Government was able to solve two problems by closing the penal colony at Norfolk Island and re-locating the entire population of Pitcairn Island along with everything they possessed to Norfolk Island.

As a consequence the surviving convicts on Norfolk Island were returned to Van Diemen's Land. And so I returned to Port Arthur.

Port Arthur Re-visited

I do not remember the names of the vessels on which I was transported to and from Norfolk Island. As I have stated previously my memory of most events in my life was good, but on both those journeys I could not have cared a jot about details. I knew what to expect at both destinations and my only interest was to survive.

On the 13th May 1850 I was back in the Oatlands district, given into service to an unsuspecting settler. What a joke, I knew the Midlands area well from my previous little jaunt there. So, from day one I knew that I would escape, it just took me longer than I had originally expected. I had almost served six years in gaol since my trial in Oatlands and had received no indication as to what would be my fate. In total contradiction to my true character, I therefore towed the line for over two years. In early July of 1852 I escaped. I was almost immediately captured and on the 6th July 1852 I was yet again charged with absconding. I received a sentence of eighteen months hard labour, my sentence to be served at Port Arthur.

Since my sojourn on Norfolk Island the Van Diemen's Land Government had learnt a new catch phrase, everything remotely attached to the government was to be made "economically sustainable". Port Arthur was no exception, and as a result expansive tracts of bush were cleared to feed the growing timber industry, large plots of land were turned over to cultivations and further workshops erected.[47]

Back at Port Arthur, and before I could serve out the sentence meted out on the 6th July, I received yet a further sentence. On the 20th October 1852 I received six months hard labour for abusing a fellow prisoner. Abusing a fellow prisoner, I certainly did. I was in my prime, strong and smart. I took what I could and I enjoyed the reputation I had gained as being unapproachable, unrepenting and violent. So when a young buck thought he could get the better of me, I gave him the hiding of his life. If I hadn't had been hauled off the scurvy little turd by guards, I would have most likely killed him. I had no regrets, in all it served me well and added to my reputation.

By 1853 attitudes towards convicts and the penal colonies were changing. So I decided to try my luck and made an application for a Ticket of Leave, this application was formally refused on the 27th September 1853.[48] If I had had any belief in the justice system by this stage of my life, I certainly had lost it by the time of the failure of my application. I would never place my faith in any system or any person again.

---

47   Port Arthur Historic Site-www.portarthur.org.au/pashow.php?
48   Toke Indent (Con 16/1) Archives of Tasmania.

Gold and Freedom

In 1856 Van Diemen's Land was renamed Tasmania and given permission to form an elected government. To hell with Tasmania, I was a free man.

I re-gained my freedom after completing my fifteen years' sentence handed down in Melbourne on the 15th September 1841. I was not about to remind the dim-witted officials of Tasmania that my sentence in Oatlands was for life.

The 1850's were a turning point in my life as well as that of the colonies in the Antipodes. Gold had been discovered in New South Wales as early as 1823, but the early finds were unofficial and sporadic. The first official finding of gold was by Edward Hargraves at Ophir, on the 6th April 1851 and the ninety-two ounce nugget triggered a huge gold rush.

The news of the discovery of gold spread like wild fire. We poor buggers in servitude were not immune to the stories. Nuggets of gold were lying on the ground just waiting to be picked up. We heard about the fortunes being made by miners that turned simple men into wealthy gentlemen. You cannot imagine the effects it had on the likes of us. Most of us had grown up with nothing and with no prospect of living a comfortable life. We never expected to escape the never-ending, backbreaking toil that we endured from sunrise to sunset. To strike it lucky would provide us with a life of leisure, something in my wildest dreams, I for one, had never imagined.

The news of the discovery of gold did not just capture the imagination of the convicts and early settlers of the colonies. It sparked a massive influx of immigrants. Prior to the official finding of gold, the population of Victoria was eighty thousand, not including Aborigines of course. The population had trebled by 1854 to two hundred and thirty seven thousand and by 1861 it had doubled again to five hundred and forty thousand. From 1852 to 1860, two hundred and ninety thousand people arrived in Victoria from the British Isles alone. Others came from Europe, America and Asia.[49]

Since my arrival in the colonies my only time spent out of servitude was in the Port Phillip District. After my removal from the District, the colony of Victoria, with its capital city of Melbourne had been established. I wondered if I would be able to recognise the town come city if I could make my way there somehow. According to all accounts Melbourne, in the early 1850's, was not equipped to deal with the thousands of people arriving daily by ship. There was nowhere near enough accommodation for the influx of new chums. Tents were used as temporary accommodation and the existence of "Canvas Town" was legalised by Governor La Trobe in 1852. The fledgling government imposed a weekly rent of five shillings per tent. Trust those petty bureaucrats to find yet another way to squeeze money out of the poor sods! The rows of tents resembled streets, and were often better signed than the streets in Melbourne. They

---

49 Gold! The Immigration Rush – www.sbs.com.au/gold/story.html

took their names from prestigious London streets such as The Strand, Bond, Oxford and Liverpool.[50]

The scene was described as:

> "One of the most striking peculiarities here to a new arrival is the immense encampments that surround Melbourne. The vast number of tents that stud the open ground in every direction conveys a clear idea of that enormous emigration to Victoria, which requires, in addition to the house accommodation of an overgrown city, the erection of canvas suburbs, where the hordes of adventurers daily arriving, may find a temporary shelter on landing, and before starting to the great storehouses of Mammon at Mount Alexander and Ballarat".[51]

It made me laugh when I heard and read such tales, my last accommodation in Melbourne was free and much more luxurious!

The influx to Melbourne was temporary, the majority of new arrivals had only one thing on their mind and that was to travel to a goldfield and find their fortune. In the early 1850's this meant trudging along the well-worn tracks and byways to Ballarat, Bendigo and the like. Able-bodied men were lured away from Melbourne and other fledgling towns.

> "Within the last three weeks the towns of Melbourne and Geelong and their large suburbs have been in appearance almost emptied of many classes of their male inhabitants; the streets which for a week or ten days were crowded by drays loading with the outfit for the workings are now deserted. Not only have the idlers to be found in every community, and day labourers in town and the adjacent country,

---

50   Gold! The Immigration Rush – www.sbs.com.au/gold/story.html
51   Gold! The Immigration Rush – www.sbs.com.au/gold/story.html – Letter to the Australian and New Zealand Gazette Melbourne October 14 1851.

shopmen, artisans, and mechanics of every description thrown up their employment, and in most cases, leaving their employers and their wives and families to take care of themselves, run off to the workings, but responsible tradesmen, farmers, clerks of every grade, and not a few of the superior classes have followed.... Cottages are deserted, houses to let, business is at a standstill, and even schools are closed. In some of the suburbs not a man is left, and the women are known for self-protection to forget neighbour's jars, and to group together to keep house. The ships in the harbour are in a great measure deserted; and we hear instances where even the masters of vessels, foreseeing the impossibility of maintaining any control over their men otherwise, have made up parties among them to go shares".[52]

Newspapers in all the colonies carried the latest news from the diggings. Letters from persons at the large goldfields were often printed. Even to the likes of me, they were interesting, including the minutest details of the daily goings on at the sites. I most enjoyed the first-hand descriptions by would-be journalists who wrote such an account as follows:

"14th October 1851
Golden Point, Golden Street Ballarat.

Mr Dear Sir- I sit down to redeem my promise of writing to you from this most astonishing place. I left on Thursday the 2nd and arrived here on the 9th, having accompanied the drays. This place exhibits the most extraordinary sight that ever met my-eyes. Imagine a small but rapid stream of water, with a very winding course, and for about one mile the banks or rather the margins on both sides are thickly studded with human beings, all males almost, for occasionally you will see a woman employed with her clothes held between her knees, rocking a cradle

---

[52] 51.Governor C J La Trobe's Despatch on the Gold Rushes

with the untiring energy of man; in other cases, two or three men mostly are employed, one rocking with one hand, while he occasionally stirs up the earth in the hopper of the cradle with the other, another for the most part, is actively employed in filling the hopper with earth and the other is perpetually pouring water with a dipper with a long handle like a warming-pan, over the earth, &c. filled in the hopper; one is sometimes employed picking and shovelling the earth out of the hole, and two more, in carrying the earth to the waterside; so that besides the enormous mass of person stationary at the cradles, there is a moving population from the various holes to the cradles on the water sides, equally numerous. Some carry the earth on hand-barrows, made of two long wooden handles and a sack sewed long-wise, on which they carry it. Some use wheel-barrows, others a piece of bark as a sled, on which they place a bag full of earth, and drawing it along the ground. Some carry it in sacks on their backs, while the tin dish-washers, of which there are many hundreds, carry it in their tin dishes on their heads; it is for the most part one scene of busy, eager industry. If you speak to a man, he answers but stops not his work."[53]

I read all the first-hand accounts and listened to all of the gossip. I needed to keep abreast with what was occurring, some day soon I would be free and I would need to decide what and where I would go to next.

Strangely the phenomena worked in my favour. By the time that I was free, labour was in extremely short supply in the State of Victoria. And, whilst the majority of the working population were attempting to strike it lucky, they still required food to fill their bellies. Victoria was blessed with large expanses of arable and fertile land. I had seen this when I was free to travel the largely uninhabited colony in the late 1830's and early1840's. Now, there were some smart gentlemen who realised that

---

53   Melbourne Argus October 1851

the chances of finding a large enough mother-load to provide you with instant wealth was slim; but if you took up good land you stood a fair chance of making your fortune and keeping it.

In the early 1850's most of Victoria's sixty million acres of cultivated land was in the hands of approximately one thousand squatters, each of whom paid their government twenty pounds a year for the lease of their land. These squatters were powerful men and like the colonial authorities were concerned about the condition of the State. Convicts made up the majority of the Australian population, at the commencement of the gold rush, and the rush potentially could allow the disenfranchised underclass to control the majority of the colony's newfound wealth. Gold caused the soaring labour and commodity prices, the abandonment of industry and the de-population of large areas of the State of Victoria.[54]

---

54 Melbourne Argus October 1851- The affect of the gold rushes on agriculture.

Mewburn Park, Victoria

Tasmania was in a sick and sorry state by the time of my release. The colony was over-stocked with ex-convicts. Served them right, the authorities were all too willing to take us convicts on as free labour, but once we received our Tickets of Leave, the "free citizens" did not want to pay for labour. Serve them bloody well right that we put the fear of God into them as we roamed the island half starved and dangerous.

This was not going to be how I finished my days. I was going to get off that poxy island once and for all. It came to my attention that Tasmania relied upon the colony of Victoria to supply nearly all of its food and in particular beef. There was no way that the gentry of Tasmania could exist without their beef!

I read with interest how the big cattle stations in Victoria could not keep their stockmen from deserting their posts for the goldfields. A Mr Johnson of Mewburn Park, near Maffra, even went so far as to advertise for contract labour in the Tasmanian papers. Now this interested me.

Johnson advertised for stockriders, butchers and carpenters, and according to his advertisements, if you met the qualifications you could sign a contract of service in Hobart and his schooner the "Eclipse" would sail you from Hobart to Port Albert, in Gipps Land, and from there it was but a short ride to Mewburn Park. Mewburn Park being situated between the Thomson and Macalister Rivers close to the township of Maffra.

I was a blacksmith of sorts and my father, if legend has it correct, was a butcher. So I presented myself to Mr Johnson's agent and with very little effort obtained a contract of service. I was forty-six years old, physically strong, a man of few words, most of them were lies, but who was to know?

I embarked on the schooner Eclipse with Walter Clare, Billy "The Groom" and Joseph Paynter. All of us had pasts that we were anxious to leave behind and all vowed that we would never return to Tasmania.

Since I had been forcibly removed from the mainland in 1843, things had changed and my first glimpse of the wealthy colony of Victoria was not to be Melbourne but Port Albert in Gipps Land. I was in high spirits and even had a quiet chuckle about "Gipps Land", named of course after Sir George Gipps, who was appointed Governor of New South Wales in 1837[55]. I had seen enough of the colonies to have a spot of land named after me!

Port Albert had been discovered at about the time of my trial in Melbourne in 1841. The discovery of a natural harbour caused a rush of development and opened eastern Victoria to the pastoralists and gold miners. Between 1849 and 1850 forty-nine thousand tonnes of

---

55 The Traralgon & District Historical Society Inc – www.gardencetnre.com.au/traralgohistory

cargo landed at Port Albert while some millions of ounces of gold were shipped out, mostly from Walhalla. [56]

Into Port Albert I came and for the first time I was free and employed. I had not made up my mind whether I would stay in this state for long. There was no way Mr Johnston could hold a man like me to a contract; but I was prepared to wait my time and see what opportunities came my way.

Now let me tell you a little about my newfound acquaintances at Mewburn Park. Firstly there was a chap called Arthur Orton, he was already employed as a butcher at Mewburn Park when I arrived in 1857. He was somewhere between twenty-four and twenty-six and quite tall, I'd say about five feet ten inches. He was a Londoner, a cockney and had a fair complexion with fair hair. Orton always wore moleskin trousers, a blue shirt and knee-boots. Like the majority of us Orton had a tattoo on one arm. I remember his horse well, a yellowish bay thoroughbred, called "Whipcord". Orton talked about Tasmania but was careful not to mention his experiences in the colony.

McIntosh, the manager of Mewburn Park, did not like Orton, he used to say that he had seen him about the wharf in Hobart Town and that "the next time I saw the animal he was walking up to Mewburn Park".[57] Orton was a best mate with a codger called Du Moulin, the two of them regularly travelled with the cattle from Mewburn Park to Port Albert. Du Moulin used to say that Orton was a dam fine butcher.

"Billy the Groom", had had a tilting match with Orton[58] and consequently they fell out with one another. I could handle Billy well, the kid was

---

56   Port Albert Photo Album – www.yarram.org/Yarram-tour/Port-Albert/
57   Notes from an old diary could be a police report book, last page shows 1876 calender.
58   Notes from an old diary could be a police report book, last page shows 1876 calender

terrified of me, and every time he was left in my company I would regale a tale or two that would guarantee to leave him sleepless for nights on those sparse and remote Dargo High Plains.

It is rare for me to respect anyone, but I did admire Joseph Paynter, later to be known as "Bogong Jack", smart and well-educated he was in many ways our better. He chose to work as a butcher, but was always aware of any opportunity to make a little extra on the side. Paynter was a good horse-thief, one of the best and he was loyal to the likes of me.

Finally there was Walter Henry Clare, alias "Ballaarat Harry". Now he had pretensions. Ballaarat Harry had immigrated to South Australia from Kent in 1846. He had brought his brother, James and his sister to Australia. "Ballaarat Harry" was the son of a blacksmith[59] he was about twenty-five years old with fair hair and whiskers, stout and roughly five feet eleven inches tall.[60] I tolerated Harry as we were both from Kent and were often assigned to cattle minding on the high plains together for long periods of time. I envied Harry; he had a fine horse and a Newfoundland dog, which was something special. I became very attached to that dog. Harry also had the trappings of a gentleman; he had a good gun, watches and money.

Unlike most of my acquaintances, I did not carry a gun. Instead I favoured a tomahawk. A tomahawk or hatchet was a very useful tool in the countryside. It was small and had a short handle and could be used in one hand. My tomahawk was my best friend. I learnt to throw it with great accuracy and could use it to cut my way through bush or to dispatch an animal. It also delivered a silent kill.

---

59   Alfred Currie Wills Police Officer Omeo letter to The Chief of Police in Melbourne 10 July 1858.
60   Henry Hill Inspector of Police Sale.

Whilst my new chums and I shared our evenings around a campfire on the Dargo Plains we found that we had much more knowledge of the surrounds than the pastoralist and townsfolk. We soon realised that we could make more money and enjoy our freedom if we left Mewburn Park and struck out into yet a more isolated area. Joseph Paynter suggested that we should go to Livingstone Creek and try our hands at prospecting and a little horse thieving on the side. Me being the oldest in the group had the most experience in purloining horses and was quick to point out to the others the large sums of money we could make in dealing in the trade. Conversely, if we struck it lucky prospecting, we could not lose. I was the first to agree to the plan. Billy, the Groom, and Ballaarat Harry did not take much persuading to join our venture.

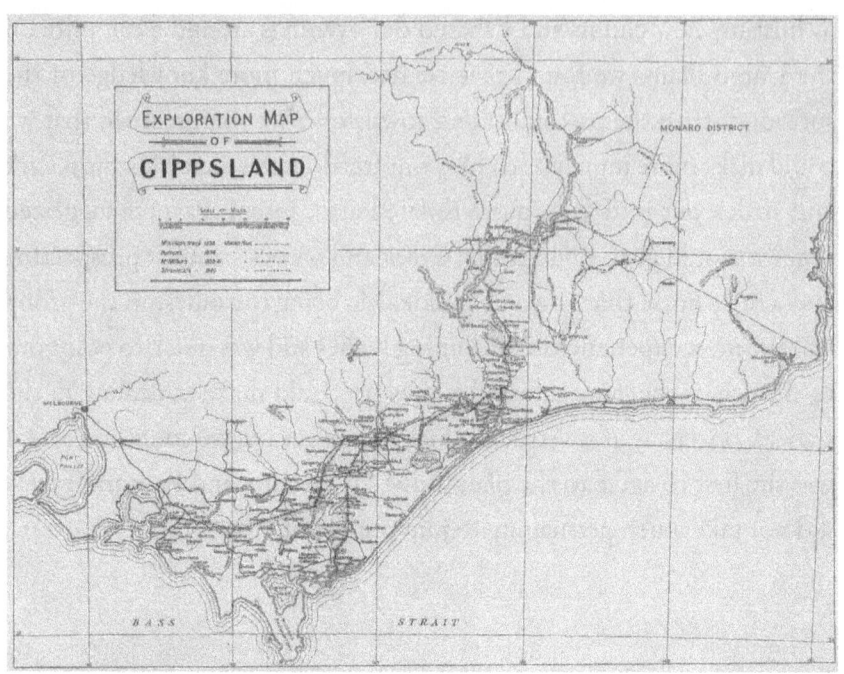

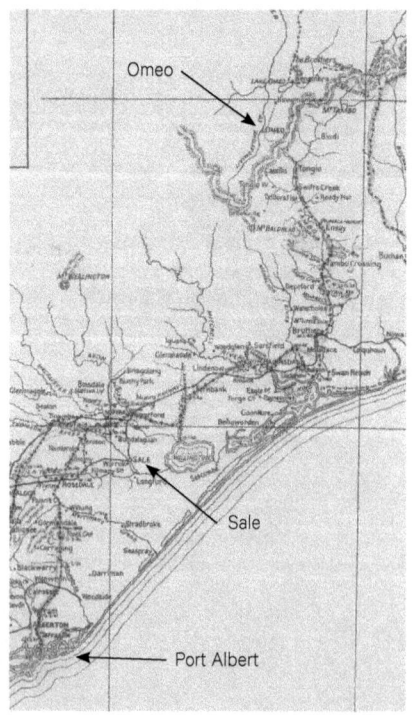

Map of Gippsland above.

Right, detailing Omeo, Sale and Port Albert.

https://nla.gov.au:443/tarkine/ nla.obj-617091118

Livingstone Creek, Omeo

Gold had been found at Livingstone Creek Omeo in 1850. Its earliest prospectors included Doctor Hedley of Sale and his partner Joe Day. In 1854 a few Californians and French Canadians, amongst them Dejarlais and Louis Hanekar, began creek sluicing near where the town of Omeo stands.[61]

> "Water races, some of them 20 miles long, were constructed and flumes built, and the results were satisfactory. In 1856 there were about 600 diggers on the field.
>
> As Omeo is 186 miles from Port Albert, it may be left to guess what provisions and outfit cost to deliver on mules and horses, over such roads as the Fainting Range and Little Dick…The individual miners often used tracks across the mountains to sell their gold at Kiewa, Yackandandah and Beechworth. The quality of the gold was not particularly high, being worth about two pound twelve shilling per once, compared to four pounds for Yackandandah or Snake Valley Gold."[62]

---

61 Recollections of Early Gippsland Goldfields – Richard Mackay p.9
62 Recollections of Early Gippsland Goldfields – Richard Mackay p.57.

So we chucked in our jobs at Mewburn Park and arrived at Omeo in 1857. I was by then forty-six years old. I immediately felt at home in this remote and harsh climate. Omeo had first been settled in 1834 but it was still quite inaccessible, remote and sparsely populated. The winters were harsh and it was necessary to travel through snow to the larger towns to obtain supplies. My past was unknown and my skills well honed.

Our gang did not strike it rich prospecting, but we found that our horse stealing ventures were quite lucrative. With few police, and those being forced to travel large distances to investigate claims of theft, it was possible to obtain and sell a filly long before the police received word of the theft. We were also prepared to take risks. We would take a horse from an isolated farm or small gold town and ride it through the passes in the mountains only we knew of, and have the beast ready for sale in Beechworth or Yackandandah in no time.

Joseph Paynter (Bogong Jack) decided to use his trade as a front and became the butcher for Omeo. Poor old Billy the Groom was not cut out for prospecting so he worked for Bogong Jack. At this stage of affairs no one suspected that Paynter was the mastermind of our gang.

Ballaarat Harry and I shared a hut on the upper Livingstone. The people of Omeo thought that Harry and I were simply prospecting for gold and had no idea that we were an integral part of Bogong Jack's gang.

All went well until Harry found a nugget of gold. As we were partners we should have shared the find, but Harry said it was his. No one was going to take from me what was rightfully mine. I could wait my time and claim my share when the opportunity arose.

I did not have to wait long. Harry wanted to try prospecting at a more remote spot, I believed that it must have been where he found the nugget, so I suggested that we went straight away as it was already mid-March and the weather would soon be too cold and changeable to travel too far from our hut. So Harry agreed and we told all our acquaintances that we would be off prospecting for a few weeks or even a month or so depending on our luck and the weather.

So on the 17th March 1858, we set off. I knew this would be a good day to start our trip being St Patrick's Day. Most of the community would be busy celebrating and none would pay much attention to Harry's and my departure. We left very early in the morning and meet no one on our travels. We travelled to Dargo and met Mr McMillan from Mewburn Park; he paid us to help out for about two weeks. Each evening I watched Harry, he began to boast again about his assets and became even more verbose around the campfire each night as we played cards with Philip Norton, the storekeeper at Foster Station.

As I said we were there for some days before we resumed our travels into Gipps Land and got as far as the McCalaster River. This was a remote and isolated area, just what I had been looking for. Harry was completely at ease and being half my age and considerably larger than me did not see me as a threat to his wellbeing. Harry also was armed with his precious shotgun. My tomahawk did not let me down. Silently and efficiently I despatched Harry to an early grave. No one would ever find his remains and I walked away from the scene a much wealthier man.

I returned to my hut on the Livingstone Creek and told everyone who inquired about Harry that we had parted at the McCalaster River and that Harry intended to go to Boggy Creek or go home to Adelaide. I let it be known that I had been quite successful and had made enough out of prospecting to start my own store and therefore had returned to Gibbo Creek to do just that. And I did start up my store and kept up my association with Bogong Jack.

What services did I offer at my store? Naturally I supplied provisions, but I also purchased gold and sold grog. What a godsend this was, it was almost too easy to extract gold and money from the green new chums. How was this done? I'll tell you.

To do a miner out of his correct price for his gold I would weigh the parcels of gold separately, or divide the whole parcel, on the pretext that the weight of the gold was too much for my scales, and then I would add up the grains and pennyweights at lighting speed, deducting at least half an ounce if not more, knowing that the miner could not keep track of the sums. There was also the trick of having glass pans resting on a piece of green baize; under the baize and beneath the pan which held the weights, was a wet sponge, which caused the pan to adhere to the baize and consequently required more gold to make it level, this coupled with the false reckoning earned me a tidy sum from the unsuspecting diggers.[63]

I also did a roaring trade in sly grog. As I've mentioned before Omeo is situated in a remote and mountainous area and it was nigh on impossible to bring in large quantities of alcohol. I was therefore able to accommodate the diggers with my own brew. Each drink cost one shilling.[64]

As a storekeeper I was considered quite respectable, until the nosy Robert James Fisher began to ask awkward questions about the disappearance of Ballaarat Harry.

---

63   A Lady's Visit to the Gold Diggings of Australia in 1852-53 – Mrs Charles Clacy.
64   Recollections of Early Gippsland Goldfields – Richard Mackay p60.

Sgt. Manson –v- Thomas Toke

On the 12th June 1858, Sergeant Manson, formally arrested me on suspicion of murdering Henry Clare alias "Ballaarat Harry" some time since the 17th March 1858.

Sergeant Manson, who was stationed at Omeo, wrote to Henry Hill, Inspector of Police in Sale a full and glowing account of his actions. He stated in his report that:

> "From information received it appeared that the said Toke and Clare left the Upper Livingstone "or new rush" diggings which is about 15 miles west from the Livingstone Creek, in or about the 17th of March last, for the purpose of prospecting on the Wentworth or Dargo, which is about 40 miles distant from where they started and over a most mountainous Country, Clare had a dog with him when leaving which was much attached to him, and in a few hours after their departure, the animal returned; it was therefore remarked by some of the remaining miners that "Clare" was done for, else the dog would not have returned without his master.
>
> Toke returned on or about the 20th of April/58 – and had in his possession the Mare and saddle upon which Clare rode when he left, and upon being asked by a miner where the latter was, replied that he left him in the bush –
>
> It being a common occurrence here for men to proceed on similar busine(s) little more was thought about it until the 1st of May last, when Toke bought and paid for a quantity of goods from Thomas Sheean of Livingstone Creek to the amount of £120.

Some of the miners on the Upper Livingstone then suspected that something was wrong, as they had known Toke previous to his leaving for the Wentworth to borrow money from Clare, to buy into a claim on the upper Livingstone and also that Clare was believed to have had in his possession previous to his leaving with Toke – about £200.

About 9 p.m. on the 11th Inst, information was received by the Police Magistrate here who after all possible inquiry being made directed Sergt. Manson to arrest the said Thomas Toke who was brought before the Court on the 13th Inst and admitted to Bail of £100 to appear on the 17th Inst.-

As this case is at present very difficult to prove; owing to the respective diggings in this locality being so far distant from each other Sergt. Manson is very awkwardly situated, there not being sufficient means on this Station to apprehend offenders at a distance or to make the necessary inquiries for conviction.

The Police horse M6 being quite unfit for a long journey and especially amongst the mountains in this neighbourhood-

Const. Dowling M16 has on the 13th Inst been dispatched to make inquiries and serve summons at the Upper Livingstone and from thence to the Wentworth (a distance of about 40 miles) to parties required to give information in the case now referred to."[65]

Well he had got the facts pretty well straight. I found it ironic that the Sergeant used his report to whinge about his horse. I could have sold him a better nag if he had asked.

---

65 Report to Inspector Hill from Sgt Manson 15 June 1858.

I was out on bail thanks to Thomas Sheean, the licensed victualler who went bail. A pretty sum too, of one hundred pounds; but Sheean had a lot to lose, I had spent up big at his store, if the Police succeeded in proving that it was Clare's money I had used Sheean may have had to hand over the proceeds.

Evidence against me also came from an unsuspected source. I have told you before that I have no time for women but I let my guard down and was flattered when Ellen Frances Clarke showed an interest in me. There was a real shortage of women, of any class or background, at Livingstone Creek and Ellen could have had her pick of any number of men, she was exactly half my age. Perhaps it was my inexperience with the weaker sex, but she shacked up with me and I stupidly boasted about my wealth and even more foolishly showed her two watches that had "come into my possession". I had even sent the silly cow to Beechworth with the watches to have them repaired. How does she repay me? She goes straight to the Police and tells them about the timepieces.

The Police got really excited about this information, as even they knew that Harry had had a couple of watches. They must have been most pleased with themselves when they received a telegram from Beechworth with a full and complete description of the watches. The Electric Telegraph was still not common in the isolated areas of the country and so a response in this form was quite novel, it was even read out in its entirety at my hearing. It went like this:

> "No information has been obtained in this district relative to Henry Clare. I would mention that the two watches of the following descriptions were forwarded to Beechworth for repair by a woman living with Toke as his wife. A Gold hunting Geneva watch No.92333 Makers name Stauffer Geneva and gold chain. A Silver hunting lever

watch No 25894 & silver chain Makers name Dent London. Will the Supt. of Police inform me if any of this property is likely to have belonged to the missing man & whether the Police here are to detain them in their possession. Please reply as soon as possible."[66]

I would never forgive Ellen for her betrayal and I would make her pay dearly for her indiscretion. But her punishment would have to wait until I got myself out of this fix. No one had delved too deeply into my past history and I could not afford for the police to peruse my record.

True to form the local newspaper was soon reporting the details of the case. My name has been spelt in so many different ways during my life in the colonies, but the Gippsland Guardian actually alluded to me as Thomas "Yoke". Apart from the obvious spelling mistake they did not do a bad job of reporting the proceedings and even made me sound quite respectable, because of this I kept a copy of the report, which read:

> "Thomas Yoke, the person apprehended on Saturday the 12th instant, on suspicion of murdering a man called Ballaarat Harry, was admitted to bail ..., appeared to answer the charge preferred against him. The case caused considerable interest, the accused being well known upon this creek and occupying a respectable position.
>
> The first person examined was Henry Wells, miner, who being sworn, stated that the last time he saw Ballaarat Harry was in the company of the accused, at their hut on the upper Livingstone, on the evening of the 16th of March last, they said they were going out prospecting, and would start about 8 o'clock next morning. I went down to the hut on the following morning before 8 o'clock and they were gone; they must have left some time, as I tried to light my pipe but could not at the fire;

---

[66] Telegram to Supt. Detective of Police at Omeo from J Sadleir – Beechworth 30th June 1858.

the Newfoundland bitch, belonging to Ballaarat Harry, which I saw at the hut the previous evening, came back to the place about 10 o'clock the same day, she did not seem fagged, cannot say how many horses they had with them. The accused, Thomas Yoke, came to my hut about a fortnight after, on a Sunday evening, he had two horses with him, a grey one and a bay one, he said he had come from Dargo that day. I asked him where Ballaarat Harry was, he said he had left him in the bush. The accused stopped at my hut that night and left the next day after dinner, he had two riding saddles with him. I knew that Ballaarat Harry had a bay mare and black foal, could identify them, have not seen them since he was missing; was a mate of Ballaarat Harry's on the Livingstone about eighteen months before this affair, never saw any nuggets belonging to him, cannot say how much money he had, our claim was not a good one, he was a very close man, but said he was worth money then, have seen a gold watch hanging in the hut, he was not a good bushman." [67]

Everyone wanted to say a piece about that darn dog. Yes, I did covert the animal, a Newfoundland was a rare breed on the diggings, but the truth of the matter was the bitch was dumb. It followed Harry around, that's true enough, but when we left our camp on that last trip it was early morning and, we assumed the dog would follow. She most probably went off chasing some wild animal in the bush, go lost and returned to the camp!

As for Harry's horses, well I knew how well they were known; and as I've stated before horse- flesh was in high demand and was easily disposed of by the gang. The gang members never questioned how I came by the animals and I didn't tell them. We knew it would be impossible to trace the horses, none of them were branded and Harry and I had worked

---

67   Gippsland Guardian Police Intelligence, Thursday 17th June 1858.

together for so long, no one except Harry and I knew who owned each horse. The members of our gang would have been well and truly qualified to give evidence about horses but none of them would give evidence against one of their own.

The Second witness for the prosecution was Jacob Woolaston, after affirming that he knew me Jacob continued on his merry way to explain that he was a barman at Day's Hotel (that's Joseph Day's establishment), he claimed that I came to the hotel about the 13th of April, on horseback. He continued to say that he thought I had two horses, a gun and a large heavy bundle. Jacob completed his evidence by saying that he knew Ballarat Harry and had seen a gold watch in his possession.[68]

Remember Thomas Sheean, who had put up bail for me? Well here's what he said in his evidence:

> "Knew Ballaarat Harry well, also a mare and foal belonging to him; saw the accused with the mare and foal at Pender's station, Omeo, about the end of April, did not make any observations to the accused about the horse, as I had not heard then that the man was missing, first heard of it about the 11th of June. On the 1st of May (T)oke bought goods off me to the amount of £120, he paid me £90 in gold dust, 25 sovereigns, and a £5 note, could not swear to the gold dust, as I have mixed it with more. I do not know where the mare is at present, but Mr Pa(y)nter, butcher, has the filly. I have not had any dealing with Ballaarat Harry for last two years, cannot say if he was worth money; he always paid his way; he was not a good horseman. The accused has always paid me for everything he got previous to this affair and since".[69]

---

68 Gippsland Guardian Police Intelligence, Thursday 17th June 1858
69 Gippsland Guardian Police Intelligence, Thursday 17th June 1858

Well you would think that I was the only one who dealt in horses! I had to mention to the court at this stage that Sheean frequently dealt in horses both buying and selling.

At the end of day one of this charade I was allowed to go at large until the next morning, under the surveillance of Sheean, who was sworn in as a special constable for the occasion.

On the following day, after a few questions were answered the case was adjourned for eight days. I was allowed bail, as I previously mentioned, but I also gave a surety of fifty pounds myself.

On Sunday the 21st June 1858 I was placed in custody, and chained up in one corner of the icehouse in the Police Station![70] Just because I had had words with Sergeant Manson, and because I was seen riding a grey mare about the town. I had then been tracked down at the Gibbo, and dragged back to Omeo by the police with special constable Sheean in tow.

On Saturday the 26th June I again appeared before Police Magistrate Alfred Currie Wills in Omeo. Like so many of my early appearances before courts of law, I was remanded. The prosecution, tardy as ever, stated that a witness had not arrived from Wentworth; so the case was adjourned until Monday the 28th June.

On Monday the 28th June witnesses including Robert Whittaker, Archibald Hamilton, Thomas Sheean and Frederick Bird gave their evidence.

Robert Whittaker prattled on about the gold nugget that Harry was supposed to have owned. He claimed that the nugget had a peculiar

---

70   Gippsland Guardian Police Intelligence, Thursday 17th June 1858

appearance something in the shape of an eagle sitting. So? Harry and I were partners and we both had an interest in that nugget. Whittaker's evidence was rubbish!

Hamilton, Sheean and Bird all rambled on about the horses Ballaarat Harry could have had in his possession. Prior to the close of the day's proceedings Sergeant Manson requested a further remand for eight days to enable a summons to be served upon John Taylor, alias Sailor Jack, as he had refused to appear before the court unless he was subpoenaed. To prove how diligent he had been the Sergeant called Constable Downing as a witness. Constable Downing stated that he had:

> "left the Livingstone on Thursday the 24th ult, reached the hills adjoining the Wentworth but could not succeed in finding the whereabouts of the parties working on the River. The person who accompanied (Constable Downing) took the poor constable's cloak and matches, putting the representative of the law to great bodily inconvenience, and causing the loss of his horse, he fortunately however, succeeded on the Friday night in reaching the station on the Corbungaree".[71]

Not a whimper about the Constable's escort purloining his cloak and matches, I note. No charges being laid for theft or perverting the course of justice. Why bother about such trifles? The Omeo Police were always single-minded. They had me in their grasp and that was enough for them to concentrate on.

So again I was remanded, until the 3rd July. No one seemed to consider my situation. Mid-winter and bitterly cold and without fire or any comforts I was locked up in the Omeo Gaol, which was nothing more than a hut. Yes, we all lived it rough in Omeo in those days, but my accommodation

---

71   Gippsland Guardian – Police Intelligence Monday 28th June 1858.

was extremely rough and again I had time to consider how I would pay back some of the fine folk of Omeo for their lack of concern for my well-being. My plans for their future kept my spirits up until my next court appearance.

Come the 3rd July, the important witness had still not arrived from Wentworth River so, naturally I was again remanded to the 5th July. I was well and truly in one of my black moods by then. I couldn't attend to the business of my store and was losing money hand over fist. If I did not get back to my store quickly someone would take my trade and even worse than this I could find myself back in some colonial gaol.

By the 5th July, winter had really set in and none of the witnesses were keen to be detained in the cold Court House at Omeo when yet again it was revealed that the prosecution was awaiting further information from the Dargo and Gibbo. Magistrate Wills decided that he would at least

Omeo log gaol

Omeo Court House

hear the evidence of the witnesses that had attended Court and so John Turner Taylor, alias Sailor Jack gave his much awaited evidence.

> " I am a miner on the Wentworth River, was mates with Walter Henry Clare, known as Ballaarat Harry at Ballaarat and the Wardy Yallock, about four years ago, we came to Omeo via Melbourne and Port Albert. About two years ago worked on the Omeo together for about fifteen months, we separated about five months ago; he (Toke) paid 5 oz to come in, he borrowed it off Harry, or Harry paid it for him, at that date I think Harry must have been possessed of about £300 in gold and cash, I know he had over 30oz. of gold dust, which he got off Sheean's Hill on the Livingstone, and about 36oz. which he got at the new rush on the upper Livingstone, he had also £27 in sovereigns and a half sovereign, we were like two brothers, we always agreed until we parted, a drop of grog was the cause of our separation: Harry was a steady man, did not like to see his mates drink....I have seen him

with about a dozen nuggets…the largest nugget he had…resembled an eagle's head….do not think Harry preferred riding to walking, do not think he would go a sixty mile journey through Gipps Land if he had a horse at the time."[72]

It was just as well I was defending myself because it gave me the chance to cross-examine Taylor, who went on to say:

"I fought with Tom the milkman, Harry's mate once when he sold out, …Harry was a close-minded man. Bill Armstrong bought the milkman out, for you: believe you were working at the Blacksmith's Point at the time. Armstrong came down to see if you would join us, you came about four days after, you used to buy goods for us at the stores when we were mates. I made a bargain for Harry's mare and foal but could not pay for her, did not get her. Harry and you worked a week together after I left. I was at the Sheep Station Hut Creek when you two went out prospecting, it was nearly two months after I had left that you and Harry went out".[73]

Yes, well this was a nice little portrait of Harry wasn't it, but Taylor's evidence did not really do me much harm. Poor Bill Armstrong (Billy the Groom) got a little perturbed. As an integral member of our horse thieving gang, albeit a silent member, Billy got a bit worried about even having his name mentioned in court. I also reckon the police were really mad about the state of their case by then, they had touted Taylor as their star witness, travelled all over the country to bring him to court and what had he said, nothing but a narrative of Harry's past few years of his life!

Archibald Hamilton then gave evidence for my defence, he stated that he had sold Harry the much alluded to foal, for the record an iron-grey

---

72 Gippsland Guardian – Omeo Weekly Summary – Monday July 5th.
73 Gippsland Guardian – Omeo Weekly Summary – Monday July 5th

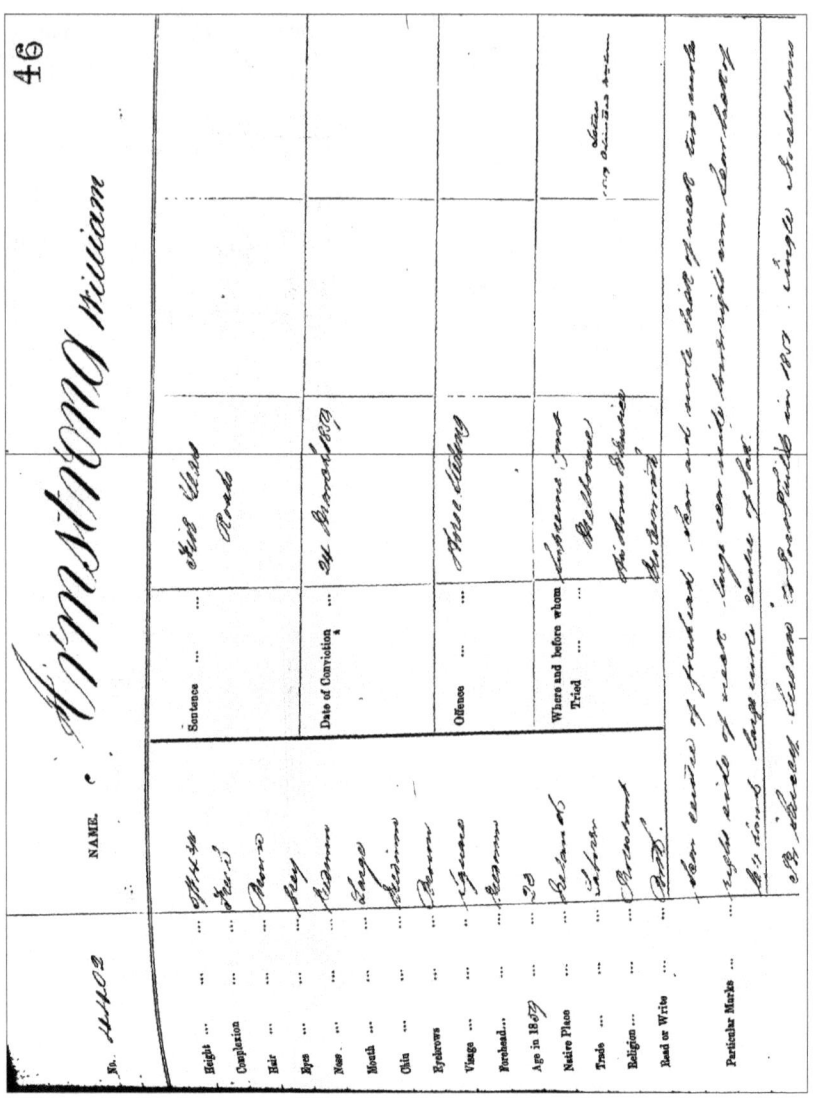

Above and opposite: William 'Bill' Armstrong's offence and sentence

colt, and that he had heard that I had traded with Harry for it. Yes, the colt was grey and yes I have told you before that I have a weak spot for grey horses.

On the conclusion of Hamilton's evidence I was remanded again for another two days. At the snails pace these proceeding were going at I would have been up for a huge legal bill if I had not represented myself; and even though no one said anything about it, I was doing a pretty good job of it.

The case progressed slowly on the 7th July. The prosecution examined their witnesses, Constable Fane, John Taylor, Sergeant Manson, Thomas Sheean and my partner Charles McDonald. Yes, my soon to be ex-partner who without a moment's consideration for my future stated:

> "I am a miner and storekeeper at Gibbo Creek; I am a partner of the accused; have been living at the store at Gibbo Creek a little over two months; remember accused coming to the store on the night of Sunday, June 13th, we had no conversation further than he said he must go back to the Livingstone, as he had got into some trouble, he took a parcel away with him, I suppose all his personal property, shirts, clothing, &c., also some rings, pepper-box pistol, and carpet bag, have never seen the said articles since he left. Understood he was going to fetch out goods from the Livingstone".[74]

Well Charles McDonald and his snooty wife would soon be ex- associates of mine and Charles would have to find himself a new line of business, because I was going to make darn sure no one supplied him with goods again. The McDonald's would soon have to find new accommodation to boot, and if they did not know it before they would certainly know in the near future not to cross me ever again.

The witnesses I called on that day included Robert Granville, Soames Davis, Joseph Williams and James George Judge.

The 8th July 1858 was a memorable day. After Police Magistrate Wills heard further evidence from Joseph Grainger, John McGowan, Thomas Sheean and Joseph Pinchin, he discharged me due to the lack of evidence. Wills was not best pleased with the proceedings and concluded by thanking Mr Thomas Sheean for the assistance he had rendered which

---

74 Gippsland Guardian - Police Intelligence 7th July 1858.

was invaluable. Yes, what a great fence sitter he was, gave his support to the prosecution and kept in sweet with me.

When all was said and done Wills had a fair idea of what was going on in Omeo and he knew that most of the miners would not rat on one of their own. He made it known that he was well aware of this and picked out Taylor for special comment, and in particular saying that his reluctance to make himself available had impeded and lengthened the hearing unnecessarily. He also warned the diggers to give earlier notice when a mate was missing and advised the diggers to give and take receipts on the sale of horses from one to another. As if anyone would take notice of his warnings!

For the record, my statement to the Court was as follows:

> "From the commencement the witnesses all state that I was back in a fortnight after I started with Ballaarat Harry which I believe there has been word from Dargo that me and the said Ballarat Harry was more than a fortnight there and then we proceeded on to Gipps Land a few days after Mr.McMillan started from Dargo which Mr.Mc Millan wanted me and Ballaarat Harry to go up the Dargo River to prospect. They all stated that this bitch was very faithful which Ballaarat Harry would not part with her for £20 which I believe it is well known from Dargo that the Bitch did not follow us a mile. During the time that we were at Dargo of the evening we used to have a game of cards playing for pistols whip coat and carpet bag with the store keeper Philip Norton of Foster Station. Then we proceeded on our road to the Gipps Land. Then we went to the River McCalaster he wanted to go one road and I another and we left the mare behind two days before we got to the McCalaster. We kept together that day as the same evening I buys the said mare for £20. We had no pen and ink with us therefore I took

the old receipts from Ballaarat Harry. In the morning we parts. Harry said he would either go to Boggy Creek or go home to Adelaide, we parted remarkably good friends. I had the nugget before we started in my possession, on the Livingstone Creek I gave the small nuggets and a specimen that weighs 8 penny weights and half for it to Ballaarat Harry, I bought it at Harry's and my bid at the new rush Livingstone Creek".[75]

Do you realise that my statement is the first time you have read my exact words during all my appearances before a Court of Law? You should not judge my ability to speak for myself by this statement. My statement may appear disjointed to you, that is because the court authorities did not record the questions put to witnesses in a Court of Law at this time, only the witnesses answers were recorded. I imagine if you have taken the time to read my story to this point in time; you possess the intelligence to guess what the questions put to me were.

By the conclusion of the case against me I was already contemplating the type of revenge I would take on all the witnesses who gave evidence against me.

Mind you I also knew that I had for once had a fair amount of luck on my side. The police spent most of their time lodging written complaints about the lack of horses in the area and requesting some fancy horseflesh so that they could go prancing around the diggings sticking their noses into miners' businesses.

The Police Magistrate of Omeo, Alfred Currie Wills, was also not adverse in adding his concerns about transportation. On the 15th June 1858 he

---

75 Toke's statement – Manson v Toke.

Livingstone Creek, Omeo

penned a three-paged letter to the Chief Commissioner of Police in Melbourne that barely mentioned poor old Ballaarat Harry. He wrote:

> "Fearing to lose a post, I have the honour to address you direct, in lieu of through Mr Superintendent Slade, and I beg respectively to request that two really good horses (Maneroo bred if possible) fit for hill work, may be supplied to this station.
>
> This afternoon I have returned from a severe journey, which ought to have been undertaken by a ...Constable, but as there was only one horse here, and that quite unfit for a hard day's work, I was compelled to travel about 86 miles, and although accompanied by an excellent bushman, a native, I was, owing to heavy fog out all Sunday night on the Omeo Plain without fire or blankets, and to-day I am thoroughly knocked up.
>
> We have a difficult case here just now of a "missing man", and there is very strong reason for supposing that murder had been committed.
>
> The Police horse now here is a thorough "screw" and quite "foundered", he stumbles and falls even on level ground.
>
> We require good bushmen here as Mounted Constables no others being of the slightest use in this part of the Country.
>
> In conclusion I would respectfully request that enquires may be immediately made (by Telegraph, if possible) for one Henry Clare, late a miner of Omeo, and generally known as "Ballaarat Harry" he is said to have a brother and sister, resident at Adelaide.
>
> He has not been heard of here since March last...."[76]

---

76 Alfred Currie Willis to Chief Commissioner of Police, Melbourne 15th June 1858

Need I remind you of that old saying "a poor workman always blames his tools"?

Like all the governmental departments I have been unfortunate enough to be acquainted with, the Chief Commissioner's Office of the Police Department did not take kindly to the demand for better horses. The reply to Police Magistrates' Willis stated:

> "I have ...sent your communication to the Supt. of Police in charge of the Gipps Land District, for his report on the matter so far as regards the un-suitability of the horse at present furnished to the Constable stationed at Omeo. I take this opportunity of remarking that my attention has on several occasions been directed to the using of the Constable stationed at Omeo as well as others from the force being employed for the purpose of leading pack horses, proceeding with miners rights to which duty can scarcely be considered as coming within the limits of legitimate police duty, and that this will to some extent, account for the horses being unfit for police work when required for it.
>
> The Superintendent in charge of the Beechworth Police District has complained of the injury which the horses of that District have sustained on every occasion of their being made use of between Beechworth & Omeo".[77]

Told you, the Police were more interested in penny-pinching and appearances than police work. Oh how Bogong Jack's gang, which of course included me, used to laugh about the appalling state of the police's mounts; but even if they did hanker for a Maneroo bred beast, the Police Department would never have forked out the asking price for such a horse. Nothing changes does it? The Victorian Government was raking

---

[77] Superintendent C M Mahon to Police Magistrate of Omeo 25th June 1858

in thousands of pounds due to the gold rush, but was always frugal when it came to spending on manpower and equipment.

There was a final postscript, on poor old luckless Ballaarat Harry. A notice appeared in the Victoria Police Gazette on the 30th June 1858 under the heading of "Missing Friends" which read:

> Information requested of Henry Clare, late a miner at Omeo, and generally known as "Ballaarat Harry". He left the above gold field in March last, on a prospecting tour between the Upper Livingstone and the Dargo country, with one Thomas Toke, and has not been since heard of. It is stated that a brother and sister of the missing man are at present residing in Adelaide".[78]

What a splendid epitaph this would have made for Harry, if anyone had ever found his body…and of course if the stonemason could have been reminded that Harry's real name was Walter Henry Clare.

---

78   Victorian Police Gazette June 30, 1858.

Life and Litigation in Omeo 1858–1859

On the very same day of my discharge in respect of the suspicion of murdering Ballaarat Harry I had to face charges bought against me by my partners Charles and Annie McDonald. Not only had Charles given evidence against me in the Ballaarat Harry case, now he and his wife were making claims for work and labour done. How did these two idiots think I could pay my debts whilst I was busy defending myself? Well that little avaricious pair were about to get their comeuppance; and how sweet my revenge was!

As I said on the 8th July Charles McDonald sued me and claimed 20 pounds for work and labour done. Annie was suing me for ten pound ten shillings, for work and labour done. I managed to have these matters adjourned (yes I had learned to use this trick in my favour). I respectfully requested some time from the Magistrate to get my accounts in order. Magistrate Wills adjourned these matters until Monday the 12th July 1858.

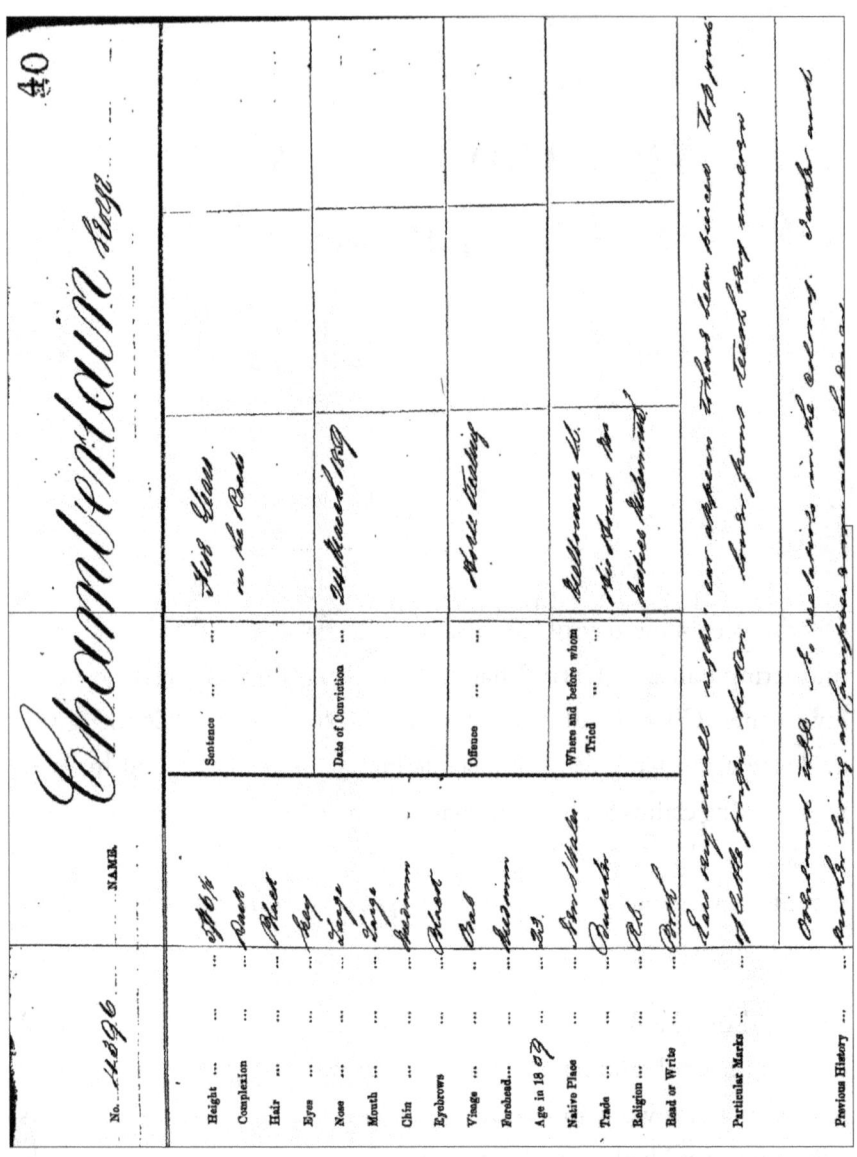

Above and opposite: George Chamberlain's offence and sentence

Perfect, I had several days to plan and execute my vengeance on the McDonald's. On Sunday the 11th July 1858 their hut along with all their possessions was mysteriously and unaccountably burnt down. Of course

I had an alibi and even if folks wanted to point the finger at me they would never make a case of arson stick. The Mc Donald's like so many of the occupants of the area were residing in a hut built solely of wood. It was the middle of winter and freezing cold, a fire would remain alight all day and into the early evening. Although most of the community were mindful to bank the fire before retiring for the evening, if you were complacent or a little the worse for wear due to a rather generous intake of liquor, and the fire was left smouldering a hut could and regularly went up in flames in no time. Mind you this particular incident enhanced my reputation as a man not to be crossed within the community.

On Monday the 12th July 1858 the cases brought against me by Charles and Annie Mc Donald were struck out, as there was no appearance by either plaintiffs. And that my friends, was the last time anyone in the Omeo district attempted to take me to court on a civil matter.

Many of my acquaintances had rather dubious pasts and had a poor opinion of the justice system. The local Magistrates' Court in Omeo was quite a novelty and my chums found that it was relatively easy to use the court system to recover money owing to them. One such acquaintance was a new chum by the name of George Chamberlain. His first sorties into the legal system occurred on the 11th August 1858 when he had two matters before the court.

Firstly he sued a local by the unlikely name of Smith for the sum of four pounds and four pence. The defendant admitted the debt and the court ordered that Smith pay the debt by weekly instalments as well as paying costs. On that same day Chamberlain also sued another Omeo resident, Hall, for the sum of fourteen pounds and thirteen shillings. He won that case[79] also and attracted my attention with his guile. It was doubtful that he made any further friends in the close knit community as both Smith and Hall had been residents of Omeo for some time and Chamberlain was an unknown.

---

79   Gippsland Guardian – Police Intelligence Omeo – August 11 1858.

Life and Litigation in Omeo 1858-1859

Another acquaintance of mine, by the name of McMahon had his first taste of litigation at the same sitting of the Magistrates' Court[80]. McMahon was sued by a bloke called Phelan for wages as a mining labourer under the Master and Servants Act. The claim was for thirty pounds, but the case was settled out of court and Mc Mahon never mentioned the case or its details again.

Not to be outdone and to all intense and purposes John Paytner was a pillar of the community. The horse-stealing racket was still doing well, but judging from Paytner's civil litigation so was his butcher shop. Bogong Jack had two actions against an Omeo resident by the name of Hall, both were for meat delivered, one claim being for twenty pounds and the other for eight pounds, nine shillings and seven pence. Both matters were settled out of Court.[81]

John had the face of an angel and a mind as sharp as a steel trap. Except for his horse- stealing associates no one had the slightest idea that there was another side to this prosperous butcher's life.

Whilst my acquaintances were busy with their civil litigation in the Omeo Magistrates' Court, I had returned to my store intent on continuing on my merry way, making sizeable profits out of unsuspecting green new chums. To my consternation I found that I now had competition.

---

80 Gippsland Guardian – Police Intelligence Omeo – August 11 1858
81 Gippsland Guardian – Omeo Weekly Summary – Friday 17 September 1858.

Mr Cornelius Green and the Case for Gold Escorts

Respectability had come to Omeo. The residents of the area had commenced to use the Courts to settle their claims and the newspapers, of which there were a considerable number, to air their grievances and concerns.

Cornelius Green

I had enjoyed less than a week's freedom when I became aware of a certain Cornelius Green. This gentleman seemed to have a particular interest in all matters pertaining to gold as well as the workings of the community. He was fast gaining respect as a pillar of society and was not averse to putting his opinions into print. The first letter I recall of his that appeared in the Gippsland Guardian was on July 16th 1858 when as a gold agent he wrote:

"A proposal now emanates from the Bank of Victoria, to purchase dust, at their Port Albert Branch, offering 75s.6d. per ounce from

Boggy Creek and Nicholson River gold; and, 68s. per ounce for Omeo parcels. It must be remembered that the price of gold fluctuates with the rates of exchange in London, and the present rates being below par, the price of gold is proportionately low. When the rates of exchange advance the price of gold will also be increased to correspond. This arrangement will no doubt be readily taken advantage of, and prove convenient as well as beneficial to all parties.

The establishment of an escort service is a very material matter, in connection with this subject as it will fully complete the arrangements now pending. A monthly escort from the Livingstone Creek (the head quarters of the Omeo district) to Port Albert would be conducted by our present police force without any great expense, and surely weekly average returns of nearly 250 ounces warrants immediate attention. The matter has already been mooted and partly promised by the Government.

The final settlement of these arrangements I am certain will vastly improve the present state of things, and its future working hailed with such satisfaction by all parties interested in the progress of the district"[82]

Pompous fool, who did he think he was, giving us a lecture on pricing of gold? Many diggers had been trading in gold for years and could teach Green a trick or two.

I was a little surprised that the Ballaarat Harry Case and Mr Green's letter could be linked together but inexplicably that is what the Gippsland Guardian correspondent did:

"The different excursions across the Victorian ranges arising from the police inquiry respecting the missing miner, Walter Henry Clare alias

---

82 Gippsland Guardian – Omeo Weekly Summary – July 16, 1858.

Mr Cornelius Green and the Case for Gold Escorts

Ballaarat Harry, will probably lead to the opening up of a new goldfield. Two parties (one of them numbering seven men) are already at work on the Wentworth, and others, from the good prospects reported, are preparing to follow:

I have not doubt but that all person in this district, and others also interested in its welfare, will justly appreciate the lucid and elaborate letter of Mr C. Green which appeared in your paper of the 16th inst., regarding the assay returns of the Omeo gold. I can assert that this gentleman has exerted himself to the utmost both publicly and privately to promote the interest of this locality, and I may add that to his exertions we are indebted for our postal and police establishments, and also future aid that Government may think proper to grant us regarding the improvements of roads, and the apportioning of the Crown Lands into small allotments for the benefit of the mining community; indeed no other single individual merits the hearty thanks and support of all classes at Omeo more than that gentleman. I have all along stated and Mr Green in his letter has fully borne out my assertion viz: that a rich if not extensive, gold field exists between the heads of Livingstone and Swift's Creek, and the country lying beyond towards the heads of the Nicholson and Mitchell Rivers...

...less crime has been committed in this district since the gold discovery than any other portion of Victoria, and this the Government knows too, or else when they granted police why did not they have proper quarters and a lock-up built"[83]

I make no apology for quoting these peoples comments, they are all long dead and I have no other way to convey to you the thoughts and ideals of those living at Omeo and surrounding goldfields. Mr "Suave" Green

---

83 Gippsland Guardian – Omeo Weekly Summary – Friday 30 July 1858

was only interested in feathering his own nest. He traded in gold and wanted protection for himself when he travelled between the goldfields around Omeo and down to Sale and beyond. This became even more obvious, as in the following months many more articles appeared in newspapers embracing Mr Green's ideas. The Gippsland Guardian was a great supporter of Mr Green and the paper continued to print articles that looked favourably on his scheme. This was most succinctly written in an article that appeared in the paper in September of 1858:

> " the Government should afford the miners of Omeo the opportunity of converting their gold into cash, especially when if done as suggested by means of the police from station to station, it could be accomplished with so little inconvenience, and without any risk. We are quite certain that the comfort of the residents on the Omeo would be much increased if they had cash to make their purchases with instead of gold in the mass. It is very likely, too, that more provident habits would prevail...."[84]

Mr Green and his co-conspirators soon showed their hands. They were going to regulate the trading of gold, which of course would be to their advantage; and to this extent they posted a notice saying that:

> "On and after Monday, the 6th instant (September), the trading price of gold dust, upon the Livingstone, will be 70s per oz., nett; and that gold dust will be taken at the old rate of 75s per oz. for all outstanding accounts up to that date for the next ensuing three months.
>
> Signed by Messrs. Day, Drevermann, Bennett, Sheean and Green"[85]

---

84 Gippsland Guardian – Omeo Weekly Summary Friday 3 September 1858.
85 Gippsland Guardian – Omeo Weekly Summary – Friday 17 September 1858.

Mr Cornelius Green and the Case for Gold Escorts

The effect of this announcement upon the miners created a feeling of animosity and a spirited determination of opposition to the scheme. I was extremely angry about this measure, not only as a miner, but also as a trader. I could not afford to pay a higher rate for gold at my store than that offered by the abovementioned. I did not have the resources to outlast them and I knew that Green, the ring-leader, would hold the others to the agreement as they had each paid a bond of £100 to observe the terms of the agreement.[86]

Not content with the alteration to the price of gold dust, Green and his cohorts continued to lobby the Government for a monthly police gold escort from Omeo to Port Albert. I don't think that the group had ever heard of the saying that "beggars cannot be choosers" as they brazenly demanded of the Government that:

> " arrangements may be made to furnish an escort of not less than three mounted constables and a sergeant of police conveying gold to the Sub-Treasury at Port Albert, leaving Omeo at a fixed date every month."[87]

Now you might ask who is this Cornelius Green? Well Mr Cornelius Green with his wife Sarah, Protestants and both natives of Surrey, England, were assisted immigrants. The Green's took advantage of a scheme to immigrate to the Colony whereby Messrs. Carter and Bonus contracted with Her Majesty's Colonial Law and Emigration Commissioners, to convey 2000 adults to the Colony, at the rate of £18.14.0 per adult. The immigrants were chiefly selected from the Midland Counties of England and the Northern Counties of Ireland and chiefly consisted of the class the Colony most required being agricultural labourers and the type of persons that were most likely to become useful to the Colony.

---

86 Gippsland Guardian – Omeo Weekly Summary – Friday 17 September 1858
87 Gippsland Guardian – Omeo Weekly Summary 8 October 1858

The Green's sailed on the barque the "Dale Park" from Deptford on the 17th March 1844 to Cork, to pick up further immigrants and then sailed on to Port Philip where they arrived on the 21st July 1844. The Green's were both twenty years of age at the time of their departure from England and were both literate. Cornelius Green was a carpenter by trade and was guaranteed employment by Mr Tweel, cabinetmaker of Melbourne at a wage of £1/5 per week.[88]

Lucky Cornelius Green, a pleasant journey and a guaranteed job in the Colony, what more could he ask for? Well quite a lot, our Cornelius was full of pretensions, so when his wife died he decided to forgo his trade and make his fortune out of the miners sweat and toil on the Omeo diggings.

I had no time for Mr Cornelius Green, but my feelings took a real turn for the worst when the bastard, not content to manipulate the price of gold, began to advertise the virtues of his business in the local newspaper. You are probably growing tired of the articles that I have quoted, but I think you should read Green's publicity and then you will be able to imagine what the pretentious businessman was like:

Advertisement
Omeo Depot
Bruthen, Upper District,
Gipps Land.

The Subscriber respectfully notifies to the Commercial Public of Gipps Land that he has erected a Commodious Building at Bruthen, which is situated at the junction of the Omeo and Maneroo Roads, and convenient to the rendezvous of the Omeo Hill Teams and Pact Trains. The want of a Receiving Store here has long since been known by business men connected with the Gold Fields and places adjacent;

---

88   List of Immigrants from Barque "Dale Park" 1844 and associated letters.

and is now opened with a view of Storing Goods, forwarding the same, and affording greater facilities for their speedy transit than hitherto arranged.

He is prepared, also, to receive Consignments, and to execute with promptness General Commission Orders.

References kindly permitted by the leading Business Firms of Melbourne, Gipps Land and Omeo

Cornelius Green
Bruthen, November 18th 1858 [89]

The final straw, as far as I was concerned was when Green, not content with being Omeo's Gold Commission Agent built a store within a stone's throw of my business, and advertised the advantages of his establishment in every town and paper in Gipps Land. The following advertisement sealed Cornelius Green's fate:

GIBBO CREEK

The undersigned respectfully notifies to the public that he has erected a STORE, and also an ACCOMODATION HOUSE, at the above place, in anticipation of the support of Travellers passing to and from the OMEO DIGGINGS.

Stores, Clothing, &c, Good Beds. Fresh Beef, &c.

Cornelius Green
Gibbo Creek[90]

---

89   Gippsland Guardian 10,17,24 & 31 December 1858.
90   The Omeo and Murray Advertiser 1 to 22 November 1858.

Dead Cocks Don't Crow

I had made up my mind, Cornelius Green's days were numbered on the Gibbo Creek and I said as much to Bogong Jack and the rest of the gang.

Planning and Executing a Gold Robbery

It was common knowledge that Cornelius Green would be taking a large quantity of gold to Port Albert early in 1859, he made this trip regularly and despite his request for a large police escort, the likelihood of this was improbable. Now I knew that Green was no bushman, could barely ride a horse and even if armed, he was no marksman. So I hatched a plan. I enlisted the help of John Paynter, his brother-in-law Sidney Penny, Bill Armstrong and George Chamberlain. We were all expert bushmen and not averse to using weapons. All of us knew the area from Omeo to Swift's Creek like the back of our hands.

The plan was simple. Bill Armstrong was already lodging at Joseph Day's Hotel, in Omeo. Cornelius Green resided at the hotel also. So Billy had to wait and see exactly when and with whom Cornelius set off for Port Albert. Armstrong was very chummy with George Chamberlain and Billy was to seek him out and tell him the details of Green's departure. Chamberlain would then alert Paytner, Penny and me and giving Green a good start, we would meet at a distance from Omeo, to avoid suspicion and then track our quarry. Once we had caught up with the party, we would conceal our identities, by covering our faces with rags, surround the party and send off a volley of shots. We would then demand that the packhorse holding the gold be left and having frightened the living daylights out of Green and his escort send their horses off on a gallop with their incompetent riders in toe. We would then take the pack horse a few miles away, divide up the gold, let the horse go and each separately return to our dwelling without any further delay. It is difficult to trace gold dust and, if we were careful not to say anything, we could wait our time to dispose of our new wealth. Green would be ridiculed for losing the gold so easily and hopefully his reputation if not his business in the area would be ruined. I had worked out an alibi for myself, just in case it was needed. I told John McMahon, who as always was down on his luck, that I could offer him a few days work minding my store as I was going to cut a road on the Gibbo. I said that I could not tell him exactly what days he would be wanted, as I had to see what the weather was like before I started the work. McMahon agreed to mind the store and said that he only needed a few hours notice. With a sound alibi in place I awaited with pleasure news of Green's departure.

On the 4th January 1858 Cornelius Green made final preparations for his trip to Port Albert. He confided in Bill Armstrong that he was no expert with a gun and asked Billy if he could load his pistol for him. Billy undid some of the screws in the pistol whilst Cornelius Green had gone to fetch some powder and caps. On Green's return Billy told him that he had lost some of the screws, making the pistol inoperative. Green was not pleased but obviously thought that no one would know that he was carrying a defective gun and was therefore effectively unarmed. Billy was extremely pleased with himself and when he attended his meeting with George Chamberlain later that day, he was able to report this to him and confirm that Green had departed from Livingstone at about 4.00pm.

Enjoying the privilege of an escort, Mounted-Constable William Greene and the company of Miss Eliza Mutter, who had recently resigned her position as housekeeper to Mr Hewitt of the Golden Age Hotel Omeo, Mr Green and his retinue were on their way. Having departed late in the day they were only able to travel as far as Burn's Tongio Inn, a distance of some thirty miles. Cornelius Green must have thought that he was truly in luck as who should he meet at the Inn but Henry Dickens. Henry Dickens was a storekeeper at Swift's Creek and

Henry Dickins

Green had an appointment with Dickens' at Swift's Creek the following morning. So accordingly on Wednesday the 5th January at about 9 o'clock the party of four departed for Swift's Creek. Cornelius Green was leading a pony on which was strapped his gold (worth between £3,000 and £4,000), Mr Dickens leading another pack horse and Constable Greene and Miss Mutter. The party crossed the Tambo River and travelled over the racecourse and when barely three miles from the Tongio Inn rode into our ambush, an area covered with small saplings, but no scrub. We had tracked them the whole way and they were blissfully unaware of our presence until there was a volley of shots. I am not going to say who fired on the party, but I must commend them on their accuracy, as Cornelius Green immediately fell from his horse squealing, "I am shot". Constable Greene received a slug in his left arm and some slugs in his right arm, lost control of his horse and was eventually thrown by the horse into Swift's Creek. Miss Mutter, silly cow, panicked, and fell off her horse in the vicinity of the Creek, but being uninjured took herself off into the bush to hide. Mr Dickens received a charge of light duck shot in the back, but as he was wearing a thick pilot coat he did not sustain a serious injury. Dickens' also fell of his horse and found cover in the bush. Unfortunately the packhorse, carrying the gold, took fright and galloped off in the direction that Dickens and Eliza Mutter had taken.

I, and one of the other of the gang advanced towards Cornelius Green, he recognised me and screamed, before I could send him to his maker. My tomahawk finished him off nicely. So, even though there would be no gold for our troubles, I for one was extremely pleased with the outcome. As our gang went their separate ways I knew that there would be no more competition for me, and my store to endure on the Gibbo.

Unbeknown to me Dickens and Eliza Mutter made their way back to Dickens' store where a messenger was immediately despatched to the police at Livingstone. By the time the police reached the ambush scene they found Cornelius Green dead by the roadside with a "fearful gash across the nose and left eye, apparently inflicted by a tomahawk, and several wounds at the back of the head inflicted by the same instrument."[91] There was little more they could do but to see the body conveyed to the Tongio Inn, and escort the gold to Livingstone.

Cornelius Partridge Green's body was taken to Livingstone, and followed by a long procession taken to the cemetery, where I am told, the Church of England service was read by Mr Venables. Ironically it was only two days earlier that Cornelius himself had read the same service over the body of James Murray, who had drowned while bathing in a dam.

I had made myself scarce and took much comfort from the fact that in a few days I could return to my store on the Gibbo and feign surprise and even outrage over the monstrous murder of my neighbour.

91　The Omeo and Murray Advertiser – Beechworth Saturday 21 January 1859.

Apprehension of the Murderers

I could never comprehend the stupidity of George Chamberlain and William Armstrong. They remained in the vicinity of the murder and eventually riding stolen horses presented themselves at my store on the Gibbo. I was outraged to find them there when I returned from my self-imposed exile. To make matters worse the authorities had concluded that I was associated with all of the unsavoury elements in the community and hence had decided to look for the perpetrators of this crime in the area of my store at Mt.Gibbo.

It appeared that Mr Day, the landlord of the Diggers Arms Hotel, had offered a reward of three hundred pounds for the apprehension of the murderers of Mr Green. Obviously Day wanted to show what a law-abiding citizen he was, but knowing the man as I did I do not think he had any intention of making good on his offer of a reward. Day was always motivated by money, after he had established his hotel and general store at Omeo, he announced and publicised the goldfield, for his business sake, even though gold had been discovered before his announcement. So he, and his party including a black fellow set out in search of the villains. Once they located the abandoned stolen horses they began a thorough search and Chamberlain and Armstrong were discovered secreted amongst the boughs of a gum tree. The two idiots were secured and brought to Omeo where they were examined before Police Magistrate Wills.

Sidney Penny and John Paynter were also arrested as accessories before the fact.

I have re-iterated the facts simply for your benefit, but I can tell you over the next few months everyone in the area around Omeo had something to say about the Cornelius Green murder. Facts were distorted and reputations made, every paper in the Colony of Victoria printed weekly articles on the topic, it was obvious that the saga, as it had now become, was just what the people and politicians of Victoria craved for.

By the time Police Magistrate Wills convened the inquiry into the death of Cornelius Green he was familiar with every party involved and had probably made some of his own conclusions before he heard the evidence.

I think that everyone was a little surprised when George Chamberlain applied to be charged with horse stealing first. Wills immediately overruled and ordered the charge of murder to take precedent.

Bloody George Chamberlain just could not keep his mouth shut, and every time he spoke he put his foot in it. Billy Armstrong wasn't much better. What idiots! Armstrong cross-examined Eliza Mutter, the woman had just about been sanctified by the time she gave evidence, and Billy queried if she could identify him. The woman had already stated that one of the murderers had a low-crowned hat on, what is commonly called a cabbage tree, and the other one had something light around his head. Billy voluntarily remarked that he had nothing on his head!!! So after the examination of just one witness William Armstrong had basically admitted that he was at the scene of the crime. And it got worse.

The wounded Constable William Greene was the next witness, and after he gave his testimony George Chamberlain piped up and confirmed that he had met the ambushed party about two miles on the Omeo side of Tongio Hill. I had known Chamberlain and Armstrong for a long period of time and I thought in my company and that of Bogong Jack's that they would have had more sense than to volunteer valuable information to a court of law.

Henry Dickens' was keen on the court recording the extent of his injuries sustained, but they were slight and if anything it just showed his true nature. Dickens could have stopped and rendered aid to the other member's of the party, but of course he put his hide first and made his way straight to his store. Once at Swift's Creek he attended Dr Fisher, who removed one shot from the back of his head and approximately a dozen shots from his back.

As an afterthought Dickens' admitted that he knew William Armstrong well as he had been twice in his service, each time for a period of five or six months. He also recollected that Armstrong and the late Mr Green had once travelled down the country with a consignment of gold and that it was Armstrong that had told him of the date that Mr Green was expected at Swift's Creek on this his last journey.

Robert James Fisher, student of medicine gave his opinion as to the cause of death of Cornelius Green being that any of the three wounds inflicted by the same sharp instrument (my trusty tomahawk) to the back of the head would have been sufficient to cause death. I was a little concerned that someone may have raised the question as to who may have been armed with such an instrument, but they did not and the danger passed when the inquiry moved onto the evidence of Joseph Day.

Now you will have to bear with me here, as Joseph Day, gave evidence concerning both of the accused. Day confirmed that both had stayed at his hotel on the 4th January, the date of the murder, and that they admitted to him that they had been on the Omeo Plains. He was then shown a single barrel fowling gun, which he claimed belonged to Armstrong and stated that it was missing from Armstrong's room the night after Mr Green was shot. Day was then shown two saddle-straps, which were found at the scene of the murder. He testified that he had sold two saddle straps to Armstrong before Christmas. He stated that he believed that he could identify at least one of straps, as it was one of the first colonial straps he had ever had from Melbourne. He had sold Armstrong the last pair as it had a cut in it just like the one that was produced at the inquest. Day then went on to state that he had frequently seen George Chamberlain's handwriting and that the hand written documents produced at the inquest were written by George.

Day was the first to incriminate Sidney Penny and John Paynter. He claimed that when he set out to track the culprits he had heard that Chamberlain and Armstrong had passed through the township and he had observed tracks of two horses, and in consequence of information he had received, he examined the tracks. Being an exceptional bushman he claimed that he recognised them as that of the horses that Armstrong and Chamberlain had ridden recently. The tracks went within a yard or two of John Paynter's house and lead away to the bush.

I was next to give evidence and I knew that I would have to tread very lightly as with Penny and Bogong Jack heavily incriminated and what with Armstong and Chamberlain being found in the vicinity of my

Apprehension of the Murderers

store and with my previous record, it would not take much for me to find myself accused of the crime. So I gave my evidence with a few embellishments. And if I do say so myself I did really well. I will tell you what I told the inquest and you can judge for yourselves.

I explained that I returned to my store at Gibbo Creek late in the afternoon of Monday the 12th January having been told by Mr Day that there were two men at my store with loaded firearms and that they had horses. From the description I believed them to be William Armstrong and George Chamberlain and I said to them "Why, you have Dan's horses," and Armstrong says, "my bloody oath we have". Then I told Armstrong and Chamberlain that they were accused of the murder of Mr Green, likewise of shooting Constable Greene. They then asked for rations and said that they meant to go about six hundred miles without stopping. I then asked them "How come it you could not get the gold; then they said whilst they were looking for Harry the Snob (Henry Dickens) the packhorse with the gold got away; and that as soon as Dickens got two charges he fell from his horse". I asked them whether there were any more in the attacking party and Armstrong replied, "We went out the night before, Sidney Penny was with us. Just about a mile or so before Tongio Station, we wanted to stick them up, but Sidney shied off. George went out and spoke with Mr Green and then we took to the 'jawed' Sidney for not carrying through with the robbery. Armstrong then told me that the next morning they tried to see Sidney, but he had made himself scarce. I then asked how they came to tomahawk Green, and Armstrong replied, "A dead cock will never crow". Then I asked George Chamberlain, "How was it he took and stuck 'em up so near Swift's Creek"? He said, "As he thought there would only be Miss Mutter, the constable and Mr Green, and they were lying in the bush near Swift's Creek where the deed was committed, and that they did not expect that Dickens would be with the party. Chamberlain then said to Armstrong "Pour into them" and they

Mr Gibbs   *Mr Macalister*   *Inspector Read*

takes and they fires, and Green fell". This was the conversation between them and me at the time, at their camp at Gibbo Creek. Then I takes and I leaves them and I comes down to my place, and McMahon tells me that William Gibbs has gone to fetch the police. Then I takes and bakes a cake. Me and McMahon were having our supper, when in walks Chamberlain and Armstrong, with the firearms in their hands. They takes their supper with us and Chamberlain then said they put confidence in me and he takes and writes out receipts, and a letter which he says I am to give to John Paytner, the butcher on Livingstone Creek, which I said I would and they said that I was not to even let his wife see me give it to him or anyone else. I then happens to mention I had marked a line from Dargo Station to Livingstone and Armstrong said; "I have a horse there, if you go for him you can have him". I told him I would. I asked him what were his brands. Chamberlain made me an answer, it was "W.P". Then Chamberlain draws out a receipt for him and Armstrong told me that when he had left to take care of his horse. Then they went to look for horses and returned and asked me if I had got a bell, and I gave it them and Chamberlain put it upon Davis' old horse. When they returned they asked me again for the paper I was to take to Paynter. I gave it to them and Chamberlain wrote on the paper and read it to Armstrong in a low voice so I could not hear. He then handed it back to me and says I'm to give it to Paynter. Then they asked for a change of clothes, and I said "There, you can go and take what you like" and they helped themselves. Then they told me bake a cake. They said they were not to be taken alive. They asked me if I had any ball or bullet mould, I said no. During the night McMahon and the blackfellow were trying to get away but the prisoners were watching the horses all night. Then on Tuesday morning, the 14th, Chamberlain came into the hut just after dawn and asked whether I had the damper made, likewise the sugar and tea, and meat packed up for them. I told them I had not, then Chamberlain asked me to fetch it to the flat at Gibbo as soon as possible. I waited some time, sent McMahon down to Green's store to see if Gibbs or the constables had come out from Livingstone. Then I delayed another quarter of an hour and I takes them their 10lb of flour, and I told them they could bake on the flat there, for there was no fear of anyone coming there. I returned home, and sent McMahon down to Green's store again, and found the Police had not even then arrived.

When the Police did arrive Mr Hill asked me about Chamberlain and Armstrong and I told him all I knew, and joined the party in pursuit taking my blackfellow with me. About forty miles from my store we captured the men, and also the horses which belonged to Mr Davis.

When the prisoners got new clothes they left their old ones in my store, I believe in my absence McMahon brought those clothes to the police. I had seen blood on the right sleeve of Chamberlain's shirt.[92]

---

92 Weekly Herald - February 11 1859 – The Murder at Omeo – Examination of the Prisoners.

I couldn't save Chamberlain and Armstrong from their own stupidity, but I could certainly save myself and I did make a good fist of it too. No one asked me any awkward questions and I made it quite clear that I was getting on in years and that both Chamberlain and Armstrong were strong young men in the prime of their lives. If folks believed my story well that was well and good. I knew that the likes of Chamberlain and Armstrong were not going to speak up against me as they knew what I was really capable of doing.

The last witness at the inquest was Sarah Muir, a domestic servant at Mr Day's hotel. Sarah gave evidence regarding Armstrong and Chamberlain staying at the hotel, their regular private conversations and then reiterated the episode as to how Billy Armstrong demobilised Mr Green's pistol.

Finding that there was a case to answer, Police Magistrate Wills remanded the prisoners to stand trial at the next Criminal Sessions in Melbourne.

The prisoners did not languish for long in the local lock-up. The authorities feared that Bogong Jack's gang might try to free them. How naïve the authorities were. I wasn't going to get further involved, as it was I was up to my neck in this affair. My past certainly could not stand close scrutiny, and the rest of the gang didn't have the balls or the brains to carry out a prison breakout. Nevertheless the police sent a large escort with the prisoners to Melbourne. The prisoners were conveyed to Melbourne in a wooden cart. Shortly after the convoy's departure the wooden cart over-turned and threw the prisoners and all of the provisions for the trip into Swift's Creek. Perhaps it was Cornelius Green's way of paying the police back for only affording him one inexperienced mounted trooper on his fateful last trip. It would have been a difficult journey on spoilt provisions. The prisoners, no doubt, would have seen this as a bad omen, Penny and Armstrong in particular where not noted for their strong constitutions.

R-v- George Chamberlain and William Armstrong

For the first time in over a decade I found myself back in Melbourne. Since I had last seen Melbourne it had been elevated to the status of a city. Gone were the makeshift housing and crude shops and stores, everywhere I looked I saw conventional housing and public buildings. The city boasted a museum and a university. There were railway lines and a telegraph service, a water supply and a town hall.

Around the private wharves and Queen's Wharf there was a substantial Customs House and the government's Immigration Depot. I was accommodated in this area during the trial in one of the many new boarding houses.

Inner Melbourne had become commercialised with merchants, agents, clothiers, tinsmiths, timber yards, brickyards, agricultural implement makers and a galvanised iron factory.[93]

---

93 Melbourne Central City–www.arts.monash.edu.au/ncas/multimedia/gasetteer/list/melbournecity.html

Banks had replaced the old residences I had known in Collins Street; and I could not miss the Houses of Parliament at the end of Bourke Street. The Chinese, had their own precinct, which encompassed the brothel quarter, not that I had any interest in the inhabitants of this area, as I have told you before I had no time for women.

Churches were everywhere. Emerald Hill a settlement just south of the Yarra River had become a separate borough and had Presbyterian, Catholic and Anglican primary schools, Protestant and Catholic orphanages and even a mechanics institute. At the time of my enforced visit, the military's Victoria Barracks was being completed in St Kilda Road. The military roamed freely and therefore I did not frequent this area.

I had little time to investigate the city of Melbourne, even if I had cared to. On the 18th March 1859 George Chamberlain and William Armstrong appeared before Mr Justice Molesworth in Melbourne's Supreme Court at the Criminal Sessions where they were formally charged with stealing two horses, the property of Soames Davis, on the 7th January 1859. Each prisoner pleaded guilty to having stolen one horse, and both were remanded for sentence.

Armstrong and Chamberlain were then indicted on the charge of having feloniously killing and slaying Cornelius Green on Wednesday the 5th January 1858.

Now you know me by now, and my past record. I was the star witness for the prosecution, quite a novelty. I'd kept my distance from Melbourne and its legal fraternity for many years, too many of them knew of my past, so before the case against Chamberlain and Armstrong even commenced I had also made it my business to see what I was up against.

My first consideration was the presiding Judge. Mr Justice Molesworth later to become Sir Robert Molesworth, born in Dublin Ireland in 1806, educated at Trinity College, Dublin and admitted to the Irish Bar in 1828 had immigrated to Australia in 1852. After a short stay in Adelaide he settled in Melbourne. Molesworth initially established a practice in Melbourne but in June 1856 was appointed a Supreme Court Judge.[94] Molesworth had married Emma Browne, who just happened to be the daughter of Sylvester Browne, who had been on the jury when I was sentenced to fourteen years imprisonment back in 1841. It seemed that I could never escape my past. I doubt the good judge discussed the witnesses in the cases he presided over with his society wife, and even if he did would a woman have any recall of her father's early life in the Port Phillip District? This would be extremely doubtful!

The Crown prosecutor was none other than the Solicitor-General himself, Richard Davies Ireland. Another Irishman and this one came with a pedigree. Ireland has been involved in the movement for freeing Ireland from British Rule; he immigrated to Australia in 1852 because of the overcrowding at the Irish Bar. Ireland had made his name as a barrister in Victoria by successfully representing the accused in the Eureka Stockade trials.

I had no idea who was going to represent the prisoners until the case commenced and I was in for a most unpleasant surprise. First up Chamberlain applied to have the trial postponed for a few days to enable him to make arrangements for his defence. Mr Ireland, true to form, objected to the wait. I grant George this; he was game and stood his ground. He spoke right up to the judge and said that a friend in New South Wales had offered twenty-five pounds to pay for his defence.

---

94   Burke's Colonial Gentry Vol 1891.

His Honour Mr Molesworth was right taken with Chamberlain and ignoring the pompous Mr Ireland offered to have the trial postponed to the next sitting so that he could organise his defence.

Rising to his feet and showing mock concern Mr Ireland said he would be sorry, especially in the case where a man's life was concerned, to throw any obstacle in the way, but in this case, not only had the prisoner had ample time to provide his defence, but besides that there were almost twenty witnesses in town from Gipps Land, and it might be impossible to get them again in a month. I had to agree with the bugger there, I had no wish to return to Melbourne again, the ghosts of my past were too close for comfort and I did not wish to give any one time to research my past.

Chamberlain was not at all put off by Ireland's fine speech and told the judge his friend lived in Cambeltown, New South Wales, and he was a friend of Joseph Day, the proprietor of the Limerick Castle Hotel, who was one of the witnesses against him. Day then jumped up and said he would pay the twenty-five pounds on behalf of his friend.

So Day paid the money over and Chamberlain's solicitor then engaged Dr Sewell as Chamberlain's barrister. Of all the rotten bad luck, it was the same gent that handled the leasing arrangement for the Kinlochewe Inn way back in 1841! He took one look at me and I knew he remember me! The bastard had come up in the world since we last meet, he was plain Mr Sewell, Solicitor of Little Collins Street Melbourne then, now he was Doctor Richard Clarke Sewell the first teacher of Law at the University of Melbourne and with a reputation for taking cases of persons who would almost certainly be found guilty of serious crimes.[95]

---

95   Argus November 8 1864 – Death Notices.

Poor Bill Armstrong had no one to help him pay his legal costs and so Mr Worsley consented to watch the proceedings on his behalf.

The witnesses, including me, then gave their evidence, just like we had done at the inquest back in Omeo. I thought I did a particularly good job and was very much relieved when my evidence was not challenged. I took my leave of the witness box to smiles and well-wishes from the public gallery.

Doctor Richard Clarke Sewell

The evidence took less than a week to be heard and on Wednesday 23rd March 1859, Judge Molesworth carefully summed up the case at great length, drawing the attention of the jury to the points in the evidence in which the witnesses agreed, and likewise to the discrepancies and then, at quarter past six the jury retired. I think the good Judge had decided that it was time to call it a day, because at twenty-five past six he called the jury back. The foreman then told the Judge that they were not agreed, but were likely to come to an agreement in a short time. Accordingly the jury was again locked up but at five past eight returned into the court with their verdict. The verdict was "Not Guilty", in regard to both prisoners.[96]

As Chamberlain and Armstrong had previously pleaded guilty to a charge of horse stealing the Judge remanded them for sentence.

On Thursday 24th March Chamberlain and Armstrong were placed in the dock to received sentence for having stolen horses, the property of Soames Davis. Chamberlain, who had retained his nerve throughout

---

96   Weekly Herald – March 23 1859.

the trial made a statement to the effect that the horse, he had stolen, had been the cause of him nearly losing his life, and he hoped the pain he had suffered would be a lesson to him for the rest of his life. He begged Judge Molesworth to deal with him as leniently as he could. George's eloquence contrasted with Billy's, who stated that when he took the horse in question he did so with the intention of keeping it for a short time only. Poor Billy, he would never be noted for his brains.

Mr Justice Molesworth, in passing sentence, said that he should banish from his mind any other charges that had been raised against the prisoners. The sentence of the Court was, that Chamberlain and Armstrong should be kept to hard labour on the roads for a period of five years.[97]

The lads were immediately taken to their new lodgings, the Collingwood Stockade. The Stockade was a prison that I had not been incarcerated in, so I was interested to hear that it had been established as a temporary prison. The increase in crime was a direct result of the great population explosion caused by the gold rush. The Melbourne Gaol was full, as was the Pentridge Stockade. The government had even resorted to fitting out old ship hulks as floating prisons in the harbour and so the government had been forced to create three additional stockades at Collingwood, Richmond and Williamstown. The stockades were reserved for those who did not have a long history of criminal activity.

Like Pentridge, the Collingwood Stockade was chosen because of its bluestone deposits, which provided a ready source of hard labour for convict chain gangs. The bluestone deposits being thick and a good quality for building and road purposes. The Stockade was erected alongside the quarries and comprised of a group of rough timber buildings. There were several dormitories in which the prisoners slept

---

97 Weekly Herald - March 24 1859.

in tiered canvas hammocks. There also was the prisoners' mess and ten solitary confinement cells.[98]

Armstrong and Chamberlain's accommodation for the next five years did not appear to me to be that bad; I had certainly endured far worst conditions and survived.

Even I had doubted that the lads would get off the charge of murder, but they had done it. Good old Judge Molesworth had been lenient and they had escaped with a short prison sentence. For horse stealing I had received a much harsher sentence and I was much older than these boys at the time of my incarceration, the justice system was getting soft on crime it seemed.

There was one final matter to be determined by the Court. Joseph Paytner and Sidney Penny were still being held in custody awaiting trial as accomplices in the Green murder. The Solicitor-General was absent from his office on the 24th March and could not be located and so the Crown Prosecutor, in a state of uncertainty, had to concede that the case against Paynter and Penny could not be heard in that session. Counsel for Paynter applied for his release. Mr Justice Molesworth replied that the application for release could not be made at this sitting. Counsel then attempted to secure bail for the two remaining prisoners, but as the judge said he had no knowledge of the nature and extent of the evidence against them. The prisoners would remain in custody until the next session when if they were not brought to trial they would be discharged.

As we were preparing to take our leave of Melbourne the first sign of future trouble appeared in the Argus Newspaper, as a codicil to the paper's report on the Green Murder the paper said:

---

98   The Collingwood Stockade 1853-1866 – www.unimelb.edu.au/infoserv/lee/stockade.htm

"In consequence of the absence of the Solicitor-General from his office yesterday, and the state of uncertainty in which, after making every inquiry, the Crown Prosecutor appeared to be placed, the trial of the prisoners Paynter and Penny (supposed accomplices in the Omeo murder) will not come on this session. The witnesses in the case will return to-morrow to Port Albert; and, consequently, if at any future period the case is again called on, the country will be put to the same expense as that which has already been incurred in the case of Chamberlain and Armstrong, who were acquitted on Wednesday last".[99]

I had hoped that my trip to Melbourne would be the last time that I was forced to visit the city.

Inspector Henry Hill wasted no time in dispatching a memo to the Chief Inspector of Police in Melbourne in which he stated that he had need of "an intelligent Aboriginal Native permanently attached to the Police Establishment in this District. When in pursuit of the Murderers of the late Mr Green, one accompanied us and was mainly instrumental in their capture, having tracked them nearly 60 miles to the spot where they were overtaken…For lack of such a guide I am constantly obliged to call upon civilians here to assist us, frequently having to put myself under obligation with, and having to divulge my plan of operations where it should be kept secret…I think an intelligent native from the "Murray" of some distant tribe would be best, especially if he was young, and had been previously living among the Whites – Half pay…should be sufficient to provide him with food and uniform which would be principally what he would require"…[100]

---

99   Argus – March 24 1859
100   Memo - Services of a blackfellow – Inspector Hill 26 March 1859.

The Chief Commissioner of Police, Frederick Standish immediately responded stating:

> "The services of an intelligent black would doubtless be of great advantage to the Police at Omeo but there are many objections to the course proposed by Mr Hill. There would be the difficulty of finding a black who combines the qualifications of being intelligent, young, and of having lived among the whites.
>
> If we were to succeed in finding such a native and were at the trouble and expense of bringing him from a distant locality, there is too much reason to think, judging from the character of the natives generally, that he would soon weary of the service, and become comparatively speaking useless, in which case we should have the further difficulty of disposing of him, for to turn him adrift from the Gipps Land Natives, who are notoriously at enmity with some other tribes in the Colony those of the Murray for instance....I therefore think the better course to pursue is...as cases occur requiring the assistance of a black, to engage temporarily one of the natives, with a promise that when no longer required, he will receive suitable remuneration.."[101]

I for one was much relieved that an Aboriginal was not going to be employed by the Police. I had had the opportunity to see the skill in which an Aboriginal could track a human or an animal and had no doubt that if one was employed to locate stolen horses he would have had no trouble in locating the animal and the perpetrator. I also knew that the natives possessed far more intelligence than the snobs and city folk gave them credit for.

---

101 Memo – Chief Commissioner of Police – 24 march 1859

A Marriage of Convenience

I had my own problem with the wretched Ellen, I had brought her down to Melbourne with me, as to leave her at Gibbo without me would have been dangerous. She liked to brag about my deeds and I could not be sure that she would not expose my business dealings to the wrong person. Anyway, Ellen had never stopped begging to go to Melbourne, see the sights and live the high life even if it was just for a week or two.

To keep Ellen away from the court proceedings and well away from the scrutiny of the authorities I had promised to marry her. The idiot was delighted with my proposal and spent her days purchasing clothing and arranging her wedding. It never occurred to her that once we were married she would not be able to give evidence against me in a court of law. Ellen thought that the reason for my smile each time our nuptials were discussed was because I wanted to marry her, after all the time she had spent with me the dolt had no idea about my true character.

Ellen planned a proper wedding and so on the 26th March 1859, two days after the trial of Armstrong and Chamberlain was concluded I married Ellen Frances Clarke at the very respectable St Peter's Church of England, Gisborne Street, East Melbourne.

Ellen, at the time of our wedding, was twenty-three years of age, and I gave my age as thirty-seven, even though I was a full ten years older. I have to admit that my age was the only incorrect information on the wedding registration lodged with the Church. I even signed my name in my best writing and was surprised to see Ellen sign her full name, albeit in a poor hand, I had no idea that she could write up to that stage. Like the fool that she was Ellen duly recorded her details, having been born in Dublin to Joseph Clarke and Mary Frances Clarke (nee Whelen). Of course we both declared that we were members of the Church of England, although I have no idea how long it had been since I had visited a place of worship willingly.

We did not tarry in Melbourne. Ellen was satisfied to be a respectably married woman. She had readily agreed that instead of joining the rest of the witnesses on a Cobb and Co. Coach trip to Port Albert and then on to Omeo; as newly weds we would travel to Beechworth instead and from there we would cross Mt Hotham, quite a sight in early autumn and then down to our home on the Gibbo.

So within a day or so of our wedding Mr and Mrs Thomas Toke departed Melbourne for the sights of Beechworth and then onto my hut on the Gibbo. Ellen was not to alter my life or my business affairs. No one even questioned our marriage. The occupants of Omeo and the surrounding district were principally male. Ellen was not a beauty, she was a complaining sow and the residents of Omeo's attention were taken up with their livelihoods and further problems brewing back in Melbourne.

I had learnt one valuable lesson from Ellen, and that was that I would never be swayed by feminie charms again. Women could definitely never be trusted. I would be well and truly satisfied with my pack of dogs and any horses that came into my possession. My marriage had been a necessity, the law did not allow a married woman to give evidence against her husband and that was all I cared about.

SCHEDULE C.

Marriages solemnized in the District of MELBOURNE

No.	When and where Married	Name and Surname of the Parties	Condition of the Parties	Birth Place
	This twenty-sixth day of March 1894 at St Peter's Church	Thomas Toke / Ellen Frances Clarke	Bachelor / Spinster	London / Dublin

We do hereby declare that we are Members of the Church of England

Married in the Church of St Peter's Melbourne

SCHEDULE C.

Registered by

Rank or Profession	Age	Residence		Parents		
		Present	Usual	Status (Mother's Maiden Name)	Father's Rank or Profession
Shopkeeper	34	Melbourne	Melbourne	John Toke / Elizabeth Smith	Butcher
	23	Melbourne	Melbourne	Joseph Clarke / Mary Frances Whelan	M.D.

This Marriage was solemnized between us — Thomas Toke / Ellen Frances Clarke

In the presence of us — [signatures]

According to The Rites of the Church of England

By (or before) me — [signature] Officiating Minister

I, **John Leopold RATH**, A REGISTRATION OFFICER OF THE STATE OF VICTORIA, IN THE COMMONWEALTH OF AUSTRALIA, DO HEREBY CERTIFY THAT THE ABOVE IS A TRUE COPY OF AN ENTRY IN A REGISTER KEPT IN THIS OFFICE.

OFFICE OF THE GOVERNMENT STATIST.

MELBOURNE. 2 4 JAN 1984

84/3605 MJH

Toke's Marriage Certificate

Politics and the Issue of Law and Order

You think that I was involved in some shady business, then I'll tell you about a bunch of blokes who could run rings around my wheeling and dealing. Collectively they were called politicians and their games began at the time of the election of the first parliament of Victoria in 1856.

The first ministry lead by William Clark Haines survived for only three and a half months, its supporters were few. Haines, a London born surgeon, who had arrived in the Port Phillip District in the 1840's was not quick-witted or a good orator. His government was unable to keep control during long debates on land policy, railways and the budget. The government's two strongest members then resigned, Stawell became Chief Justice and Childers sailed home to England in the belief that he would become Agent-General. The appointment never eventuated. On the 3rd March 1857 Sladen, a member of Haines' Ministry made a tactless comment regarding the manner in which he proposed to apply the vote for immigration purposes. Even moderate politicians took umbrage to Sladen's comment and the opposition through John O'Shanassy and Archibald Michie swooped. Haines resigned and a week later John O'Shanassy, the elected member of the Legislative Assembly for Kilmore, announced his cabinet to the Assembly.

John O'Shanassy was born near Thurles, Tipperary, Ireland in 1818; he had little schooling and migrated to Melbourne in 1839. He tried farming for a few years, returned to Melbourne and in 1845 opened a draper's shop in Elizabeth Street;[102] he was often referred to as an "Irish papist demagogue draper".

O'Shanassy's cabinet was far from attractive, Foster was appointed Treasurer and by all and sundry was considered finished as a politician. Augustus Greeves was a bonded storekeeper and had a reputation for being shifty, Henry Samuel Chapman was not popular with the public and "Richard Davies Ireland, spendthrift, careerist and the terror of judges in court"[103] together with his leader, O'Shanassy, provoked the anti-Catholic supporters in the community.

O'Shanassy's ministry lasted a few weeks only and was displaced by Haines' second government, which had a strong squatting, agricultural and mercantile interest. Haines' government failed again and was replaced by another O'Shanassy ministry, which was financed and capital based. Charles Gavan Duffy, yet another Irish patriot and G.S.Evans had no business interests but all the other ministers were directors of banks or of insurance, mining and suburban railways companies. Miller, Harker and Chapman, all minister, launched the Victorian Life and General Insurance Company. The ministry was in fact very energetic in their self-advancement.

With brawling and allegations of malpractice and "with a government bankrupt of policy, powerless, and suspect of continually advancing their

---
102 Dictionary of Australian Biography.
103 The Golden Age- A History of the Colony of Victoria 1851-1861 – Geoffrey Serle.

private business interests, and a conservative Opposition with no better policy than to fan the flames of religious hatred"[104] the first parliament of the State of Victoria came to a close.

The conservative opposition to O'Shanassy formed a Constitution Association under William Nicholson and in May 1859 and June 1859 its members began a campaign against O'Shanassy's government which centred on corruption, patronage to its supporters, minister's characters, administrative decision and law and order.[105]

Now folks like me residing in and around the Omeo area had no real idea about what this parasitic bunch of hypercritical and bureaucratic bunglers were doing in Melbourne. Most of us had never had the right to vote in any form of elections before and complain as we frequently did about our lot in life, there was not much that we could do about it until this time. It seemed though that city folk had taken to the game of politics more than we had in our remote community, and so before the folks in and around Omeo knew it, the outcome of the case of Chamberlain and Armstrong became an example of the O'Shanassy government's corruption and ineptitude of its ministers.

I had returned to my store on the Gibbo, by the time trouble began to brew back in Melbourne. My attention was eventually drawn to the problem that this political turmoil would cause me. The government's handling of law and order issues were reported and condemned by every paper in the State of Victoria, with no exception. The abuse and criticism came from politicians and the public at large. Not a week went by without some article appearing in a paper or journal about the government and it's handling of the Chamberlain and Armstrong trial. I shan't bore you

---

104 The Golden Age- A History of the Colony of Victoria 1851-1861 – Geoffrey Serle
105 The Golden Age- A History of the Colony of Victoria 1851-1861 – Geoffrey Serle

with numerous examples of the type of articles circulating at the time. Instead I will quote one article only, which captures the mood of the times perfectly. The article appeared in the Weekly Herald under the heading of "Criminal Justice and the Government' and it went like this:

> "It is beyond all question that the most serious and even ruinous charge which can be brought against the government is the charge of incompetence or wilful error, in the exercise of that branch of its functions which included the administration of criminal justice. What interest of a community is safe if life and property be insecure? And life and property are undoubtedly insecure in a country where the Executive is accustomed to deal out criminal justice in capricious and unequal manner. This is the dreadful charge to which we are sorry to say, our present Government has exposed itself. This is the alarming condition into which its persistent maladministration has at length plunged the country.
>
> Within a brief period public attention has been powerfully arrested upon two conspicuous criminal cases, both involving murders of peculiar atrocity, in which the action of the Government has been of a specially objectionable kind. We allude to the cases of Regan[106] and the two Omeo murderers. In the first, the Government saw fit to exercise a leniency for which there was no conceivable reason nor defence. In the second, two culprits, to whom the capital crime of which they were accused has been subsequently brought home, were certainly assisted to evade the justice of the law, by an act of sheer negligence on the part of one of the Law Officers of the Crown. These cases – it is useless to deny it – have made a most profound impression on the public mind. But a third similar case has just arisen of a character so appalling that it completely flings the two former in the shade. Of course we

---

106 Weekly Herald- July 8, 1859

refer to the case of a man Neale, who was falsely accused of murder at Jones' Creek[107] and to the shocking misconduct of the Government in relation to this deeply injured man, from the commencement to the end of the very remarkable affair.

We take it for granted that our readers are fully acquainted with the circumstances of the matter in question. If they are not, we refer them to the two articles on the "Jones Creek Murder," in the Mount Alexander Mail and the Maryborough Advertiser. Now, the one grand specialty in the connection between this case of Neale's and the Government is the fact, that here the latter is found throwing all its weight, - and carefully going out of its way to throw all its weight, - into the scale against an innocent man whose life is put in jeopardy by the villainy of a gang of perjured conspirators! Neale is accused of the double murder at Jones' Creek, and before he is called on to produce his rebutting evidence it comes out that the whole charge is a satanic concoction, and that at the time the murders were perpetrated he was a thousand miles away. But the unfortunate and culpably stupid administrators of justices at Dunolly at once assume the guilt of the accused man, - take every pains to prevent his adopting any means to establish his innocence, - absolutely deny his legal adviser access to him, - further refuse to send a simple telegraphic message, which of itself would have been sufficient to establish the naked falsity of the atrocious charge made against Neale – allow the perjured conspirators the fullest facilities for concocting their horrible plot, - and, when the case comes on for trial, use all their power to procure Neale's conviction!

Thus the unaccountable and causeless leniency shown to Regan, and the negligence evinced at the first trial of Armstrong and Chamberlain, are balanced by the exhibition of something like a furious eagerness

---

107 R-v- Job Neil July1859.

to procure the conviction of a man, whose innocence was so evident that the slightest reasonable attention to his own simple story was quite sufficient to prove it! Such is the manner in which our present Government conducts the most important branch of its functions. But really this cannot be endured any longer. This is – to quote a characteristic phrase of Curran's – this is "playing nine-pins with the lives of men!" We prefer to leave the plain narrative to carry its own moral with it to the minds of our readers, rather than endeavour to enforce it by arguments which must of necessity weaken its intrinsic strength. We have only to ask, in blank amazement, what the Government means now to do in this terrible business? What is to be done with Mr Furnell? And when he is disposed of – as we shall suppose he must be, in some way or other – what is to become of the Government which administers criminal justice in the manner we have here exhibited?"[108]

O'Shannassy and his cronies were intent on keeping their positions of power and so they were forced to act and in an attempt to placate the public at large decided that they would make an example of George Chamberlain and William Armstrong. The first I heard of this new turn of events was when I was subpoenaed to appear as a prosecution witness for the case of Regina-v- Chamberlain and Armstrong. This time the boys were to be charged with shooting at Constable William Greene, with the intent to kill.

---

[108] Weekly Herald – July 8 1859.

The Second Trial, of Chamberlain and Armstrong.

The newspapers were baying for blood by the commencement of the lads' second trial. It had nothing to do with evidence; the trail was all politically motivated. I would have had a clear conscience about its outcome if I had a conscience.

The papers no longer referred to Chamberlain and Armstrong by name, they were simply referred to as "murderers". The boys had commenced their sentences for horse stealing when once again the seventeen witnesses from Omeo and surrounding areas were brought down to Melbourne.

The mood of the press and the public became very obvious to the witnesses on our arrival in Melbourne. Trooper Greene had played a very small part in Armstrong and Chamberlain's initial trial. No one had spared any sympathy for the young officer at the time. Now, courtesy of the numerous newspaper reports, everyone was aware that George and Billy were being tried for the shooting of Trooper Greene with the intent to murder him. Owing to the wounds sustained by Greene, he was now classified unfit for service and after the trial was to be dismissed from the police force with twelve months pay.

Trooper William Henry Greene was born in 1837 in Shinrome, King's County Ireland. Initially he went to South Australia with his parents in 1848 and resided in Hindmarsh for a few years. In 1852 Greene's father opened a store at Golden Point, but eventually the family returned to Ireland.

In Ireland William Greene enlisted as a Lieutenant in the South Cork Rifles, but found this not to be to his liking and returned to the Colony of Victoria in 1858.[109]

The trooper's role in the failed robbery had suddenly been elevated and Greene, now aged twenty-two, was being described as courageous and a fine young gentleman.

Mr Ireland's reputation was in tatters thanks to the campaign waged by the papers and the governmental opposition. Solicitor-General Ireland needed to assume a very high profile in this case. The Crown had to prove its' case if he was to have any chance to resurrect his political career. Of course the charge against Chamberlain and Armstrong was a capital offence so if the Crown succeeded in proving the charge Chamberlain and Armstrong would hang.

On Wednesday the 29th June 1859, in the Supreme Court at Melbourne George Chamberlain and William Armstrong pleaded not guilty to the charge of shooting at William Greene, a mounted constable, with intent to murder him on the 5th January 1859. The prisoners, in order to make them more identifiable, were dressed in the clothes in which they were arrested, in accordance with the instructions of Solicitor-General

---

[109] Sale Newspaper circa 1918

The Second Trial, of Chamberlain and Armstrong.

Richard Ireland. Chamberlain and Armstrong would otherwise have appeared in prison clothing.[110]

This was the second time in just a few months that I had been subpoenaed to give evidence in the Supreme Court of Victoria. The Court consisted of a stone building, which had been erected in 1842-43 and two wooden courtrooms built in 1853. The Court was situated on the northwest corner of La Trobe and Russell Streets and was, in everyone's opinion too far away from the commercial centre of Melbourne and from public transport.[111]

The presiding judge, at this trial was Mr Justice Pohlman. R.W.Pohlman was a prominent personality, and a straight-laced wowser. Pohlman had been an official adviser to Governor La Trobe and was nominated to the Legislative Council as a government spokesman. In 1855 Judge Pohlman had become the President of the Society for Early Closing, a society, which was formed to encourage shopkeepers to close their business at six o'clock. Of course the Society did not succeed in achieving its' aim. When the Evangelical Alliance was formed in 1857, Pohlman was elected as the president. The Alliance emphasised sabbatarianism bordering on the fanatical and caused an outcry when the government allowed trains to run on Sundays. The Alliance was also behind the prevention of hotels being opened on the Sabbath.[112] So Pohlman was in every respect a very straight-laced Victorian gentleman.

At this, their second trial, Armstrong and Chamberlain were both to be represented by my nemesis Dr Sewell. Sewell knew from the onset of the trial that the prosecution would place every obstacle in his path to prevent the defendants from receiving a fair trial. In fact even before one shred of

---

110 Ovens & Murray Newspaper June 30,1859
111 Supreme Court of Victoria _ About the Court History – www.supremecourt.vic.gov.au
112 The Golden Age – A History of the Colony of Victoria 1851-1861- Geoffrey Serle.

evidence had been heard Sewell was on his feet attacking the prosecution for failing to furnish him or his instructing solicitor, Mr Frank Stephen, with details of the fresh evidence the Crown claimed to adduce at the trial, and further stated that the defence had only been supplied with a list of the names of the witnesses to be called by the Crown a few hours before the commencement of the trial. Sewell looking me straight in the eye said, 'and some of the witnesses, were the very dregs of society".[113] Sewell continued by stating that he would not lend himself to a mockery of a trial and that he would not be a party to a judicial murder.

The Solicitor-General. Mr Ireland, slowly rose to his feet, and with a most angelic smile on his face said, "Well now, after that little bit of a theatrical display, I can assure you that there has been no suppression of the case. I directed a notice of trial, to be served on the prisoners, and that this notice was read to them by an officer of the Penal Department on the 26th May. The officer asked the prisoners if they were willing to be tried, and they not only said that they were, but that they wished it!"[114]

The bickering between Sewell and Ireland seemed to go on for a very long time; until I think even the Judge himself had had enough. Dr Sewell was then offered an adjournment of three days, so that he could obtain copies of the new evidence and have the opportunity to peruse it. It was therefore arranged that the trial should be postponed until the Friday, but as Friday was a holiday, being the anniversary of Separation Day, His Honour left the date of the commencement of the trial to be arranged with the Crown Office.

It seems to me that at the commencement of every court action there must be an adjournment. So again I had to cool my heels in Melbourne

---

113 The Ovens & Murray Advertiser Monday 27 June 1859
114 The Ovens & Murray Advertiser Monday 27 June 1859

The Second Trial, of Chamberlain and Armstrong.

for the best part of a week. I had to re-think my evidence, because although I was the star witness for the prosecution, Sewell knew my record and was preparing to expose my history to the jury.

I also knew, as did everyone involved in this case, that the tenor of the trail would be entirely different to the initial inquest and original trial. For starters Eliza Mutter had returned to England and as both Constable Greene and Henry Dickens' had been wounded and did not see their assailants, there would be no evidence that could place the defendants at the scene of the crime. The only circumstantial evidence would be the cut riding strap which was found in the vicinity of the murder, which Joseph Day would swear was the strap or a similar one to the one he sold Armstrong.

More emphasis was to be placed on John McMahon's evidence and the Crown would also produce more witnesses who were willing to swear that the handwriting on the alibis given to me to be passed on to Joseph Paynter were written by Chamberlain and Armstrong. This was of vital importance to the Crown's case, as the prosecution would argue that if Armstrong and Chamberlain were not guilty of the crime, why would they be requesting alibis? Secondly, even though I had claimed to be the recipient of the written documents, I had sworn that I was illiterate. Not true of course, but essential for my wellbeing. Mind you I blame the defence for not checking my evidence. I was right pleased that Chamberlain and Armstrong did not know that I could read and write and that no one tried to ascertain if my statement was correct.

Finally the Crown was going to rely upon evidence given by police officers, always a good stand-by. The naive public would never consider that a police officer could be anything but trustworthy. In this case however the Crown would rely upon the police's evidence in respect of the capture of Chamberlain and Armstrong.

The Crown's case was basically uncorroborated and circumstantial, laced with many references to law and order and much empathy for the ruination of a young police officer's career.

The Crown went to great lengths to locate John McMahon, who having given his evidence at the first trial had made a hasty departure from Melbourne. McMahon was smart enough not to return to the Gibbo, he knew my reputation and he also knew the members of the horse stealing gang. One of us would have ensured that McMahon made a timely disappearance if he had returned to our patch. So no one knew exactly where he had taken up residence and it took the Victorian Police much time and manpower to locate him. Eventually, McMahon was located in Back Creek, near Yackandandah by Constable White. McMahon and Constable White travelled in style in a Cobb and Co. Coach to Melbourne in order to arrive just in time for the commencement of the trial.

Cobb and Co. had quite a reputation in the Colony of Victoria. It was the most successful company of its' kind at this time and pioneered transport routes and delivered mail, gold and passengers throughout the country. The company was set up in Melbourne in 1853 by a small group of Americans, Freeman Cobb, John Murray Peck, John B Lamber and James Swanston. Cobb and Co. was so successful that in May 1856 it was sold for sixteen thousand pounds to Thomas Davies.[115]

Inspector Hill, police officer in charge of the Livingstone Police Station, also arrived in style. Travelling from Port Albert to Melbourne on the

---

115   A Brief History of Cobb & Co –www.cobbandco.net.au/History –of-CobbCo.html

steam ship "Shanter". Hill was anxious to impress, having no intention of remaining at Livingstone where the majority of his time was spent writing to his superiors requesting supplies and justify his lack of success in suppressing the horse stealing gang on his patch.

On the 1st July 1859 George Chamberlain and William Armstrong were placed in the dock and the Jury empanelled. Immediately Dr Sewell was on his feet complaining that one of the Jury had performed similar duty when the prisoners were formerly tried. The Judge looking down at the defence's counsel, without a moment's hesitation stated, that he did not feel justified in relieving the Juryman from his duty. Pohlman attempted to justify his reasoning. He stated that the prisoners, in the former trial were charged with a capital offence, the attempt to commit murder, but this case was different, the charge had been narrowed to shooting with intent to kill and murder.

I could have told you there and then that Chamberlain and Armstrong were done for. It was obvious that nothing would stand in the way of their conviction this time. So I thought to myself, that there was no way that I would hold back. I had to be extremely cautious and cunning to ensure that I did not find myself incriminated in any way.

The Solicitor-General with a great show of compassion and understanding called William Greene to the stand. Without any show of emotion the officer recited his prepared statement. In a clear and strong voice he stated that:

"I am a mounted trooper and on the 4th January at 4 o'clock I started from the Police Station at Livingstone Creek escorting the late Mr Green and Miss Mutter. Mr Green was leading the party. We went twelve miles that evening and stopped at Burn's Inn on the Tongio Creek. At about 5.30 p.m. we were about two miles from Burn's Inn when we encountered three men riding on horseback in the opposite direction to our party. One of the men was a stranger, but I recognised both Sidney Penny and George Chamberlain. George rode up and shook hands with Miss Mutter and spoke to her, whilst the other two men rode off.

On Wednesday the 5th January Mr Green, Miss Mutter, the store-keeper Dickens and I had travelled about three miles in the direction of Swift's Creek when I heard a shot fired, not knowing where it came from, I looked ahead and saw Mr Green turn his head to his left then a man stepped out from behind a tree to the right, pointing a double-barrelled gun at me. The man fired the gun and I felt wounds in both arms and my horse bolted four yards to the left. I saw another man fire again, this man was not tall and was wearing a dark shirt. Our assailants had light coloured horses. I then saw another person run in the direction where I afterwards found the deceased, but I could not identify this man. A second shot was then fired and my horse jumped into the river and I was thrown off. I managed to mount my horse and ride back to Burn's Inn where my wounds were dressed. I then returned to the scene of the attack, with a man named Cross, and found the body of Cornelius Green. Mr Green's body was lying face down in a pool of blood. I also found two leather straps, which were lying near the tree where the man had stepped out from and fired at me."[116]

Henry Dickens then gave his evidence, stating that:

> "I saw Armstrong on Sunday the 2nd January and he told me that Mr Green, the goldbroker and commission agent, would be out to see me on the Wednesday. I am not aware that Armstrong ever brought any other messages from Mr Green.

---

116 Argus –July 1, 1859

The Second Trial, of Chamberlain and Armstrong.

I saw Mr Green, the Trooper and Miss Mutter at Burn's Inn on the following Tuesday evening. The following morning at about 9.30am we started off towards my store. I had a lead horse, Mr Green also had a horse that carried gold. Mr Green and Miss Mutter rode ahead of me and the mounted constable, Greene, was behind when we were attacked and I was shot in the back causing my horse to bolt. I eventually gained control of my mount and located Miss Mutter hiding in the bush. We then proceed to my inn for assistance."[117]

John Mc Mahon was next to give his evidence, and he held that the prisoners had arrived at my store at Gibbo Creek on the 8th January, three days after the murder of Cornelius Green, whilst I was at Livingstone Creek and that they had guns with them. Mc Mahon said that Chamberlain and Armstrong had stayed at my store until the 11th January and that during this time Chamberlain wrote a letter. He further stated that on the day that the pair left the Gibbo they changed their clothes and left their old clothes behind. McMahon was adamant that there was blood on Chamberlain's old shirt and hat.

The Solicitor-General then showed McMahon the guns that were found on the stolen horses and McMahon swore that they were similar, but that he could not be sure, that they were those belonging to Chamberlain and Armstrong.

McMahon was then cross-examined at length by Dr Sewell. I do not know who was more relieved, he or I when at last he stepped down from the witness box.

My relief was short-lived, as I was the next witness to take the stand. I knew that I had to be on my guard to survive this trial unscathed.

---

[117] Argus – July 1, 1859

The Solicitor-General, Mr Ireland, was kind to me, after all I was his star witness. He lead me through the evidence I had previously given in Chamberlain and Armstrong's first trial, and then asked me point blank if the defendants' had admitted to killing Cornelius Green. I replied, " I asked them why they had tomahawked him; and Armstrong replied "A dead cock will never crow". This statement had just as good an impact on the jury as it had had in the defendants' first trial. There was an audible gasp from the gallery of spectators and I could feel the jury's gaze growing more and more intense upon me as I continued to say " I asked them why they didn't get the gold, and they said whilst they were looking for Harry Dickens, the packhorse got away. They also told me that the evening before the deed was committed they had intended to rob Green, both prisoners said this. The defendants also told me that there were three of them in their party and that the third member of the party was Sidney Penny. The defendants told me that they would have had the gold that evening if it had not been for Sidney Penny, because as they had approached Green's party, Penny had shied off and would not have anything else to do with the robbery."

I continued my rehearsed evidence by stating that I had found the prisoners in the neighbourhood of my store when I had returned from Livingstone, on the 10th January. I re-iterated how I had seen Chamberlain write portions of a document which I was instructed to hand to a man named Paynter, in whose employment Chamberlain was in as a butcher. I confirmed that I could not read, and only knew the letter "T" as in Thomas and Toke, so I did not know what was in the letter. Instead of giving the letter to Paynter, I of course handed in to Inspector Hill. On reading the letter Inspector Hill had told me that the letter was telling Paytner what he and Sidney Penny were to swear to in case the defendants were arrested for the commission of the crime.

The Second Trial, of Chamberlain and Armstrong.

I had thought that John McMahon had a tough time fending off the questions put to him by Dr Sewell, but that was nothing to what I had to withstand.

Sewell rose slowly to his feet and looking me straight in the eye asked me if I had been transported and had been imprisoned in several gaols. The gall of the man! I had to think fast .I said "I came from England, I was transported and I will not answer you for this until the case is determined. I decline to answer whether I was accused of any other crime in England than that for which I was transported. I decline to answer how many gaols I have been in". Sewell was not perturbed and then implied that I had been brought before a magistrate for the murder of Ballaarat Harry, and that Harry was last seen in my company, and that some time later I had returned to my home with Ballaarat Harry's horse, dog and a gold nugget. Bloody barrister, he had done his homework on me. But true to form, I remained calm and eventually the Solicitor-General came to my aid reminding the Court that I was not on trial rather Dr Sewell should remember who the defendants were and that he should not attempt to undermine my character.

I can tell you that by the time I stepped down from the witness box I had truly had enough of this trial and the characters involved within it. I wished that I could escape the courtroom and the City of Melbourne and return to the isolation of my patch at the Gibbo.

Soames Davis then took the stand and related how on the 10th January he had tracked down two persons who had stolen his horses. He stated that before he and his companions could catch the guilty parties, the horse thieves had become bogged in the scrub and had abandoned the horses. Davis stated that he found two guns in one of the saddlebags. Soames also stated that he was familiar with Chamberlains writing. Davis was then shown the letter that I had handed to Inspector Hill. He claimed he could not be sure it was Chamberlain's writing.

The six fresh witnesses then gave their evidence in quick succession. First in the dock was none other than Inspector Hill. He described the search for the prisoners and then in detail stated that, "when I apprehended the defendants they said "On which charge do you arrest us?" I asked a question in return, 'Do you have stolen horses in your possession?' The defendants said "Yes" and appeared to be pleased as they thought that was all I would charge them with. I then asked the defendants if they expected any other charge to be made against them. Neither defendant replied. The defendants were then searched by Constable White, who found a gun and revolver in the defendants possession."

Constable White followed his superior into the witness box and in a short and concise statement explained how he had searched the defendants and the results of his search.

Mr Bennet then swore that he had sold William Armstrong some caps of gunpowder four weeks prior to the murder of Cornelius Green and that he was familiar with George Chamberlain's writing. When shown the alleged alibi Bennett claimed that it was in Chamberlain's writing because of the way the letters "b", "g" and "p" were written.

Next witness was the newsagent at Livingstone Creek, William Crimp, who stated that he knew both prisoners by sight and that he was familiar with Chamberlain's writing, as Chamberlain had written his butcher's receipts for him. Crimp swore that he was in no doubt that the writing on the document shown to him was that of Chamberlain's.

Gibbs then came to the witness box and explained that seven days after the murder of Cornelius Green, he had travelled a distance of thirty miles from his workings at Gibbo, to Police Headquarters at Livingstone to advise Inspector Hill that the two defendants had been seen at Toke's store procuring rations and that he had waited until it was dark to make his escape and to alert the police of the whereabouts of the murderers.

Finally John Wright, who was a member of the Mining Board, swore that McMahon had come to him about the defendants, and that he had consequently despatched Gibbs to the Police Headquarters to alert the Police of the whereabouts of Chamberlain and Armstrong.

The examination of the witnesses lasted until five o'clock, after which Dr Sewell addressed the jury for nearly two hours in defence of the prisoners. In the course of his remarks Sewell attributed the prisoners being again placed on trail to the abuse of the press, by the former acquittal being made a ground of launching political animosity. He paid a high tribute to the bravery of Trooper Greene and appealed to the religious and humane sympathies of the Jury on behalf of the prisoners. Sewell then unleashed the following tirade, which was also published in the newspapers the following day in its entirety:

> "I alluded just now to the peculiar circumstance under which this case had come before the court. The Solicitor-General indeed has also referred to the proceedings in the former trial…After an acquittal on a former charge – a charge essentially in all its main facts identical with the present – and which has been investigated before twelve men, .announced a verdict of Not Guilty.… I do not believe that the case would ever have been brought before you again. The prisoners have already been acquitted on that charge…It is notorious that political and party feeling had laid hold of the result of the last trial and kept alive an excitement which in the ordinary course of proceedings in a Court of Justice, would have died away. I believe this case would never

have been revived, if political animosity most unproper and most unjust grounds for attacking the present Government...The whole country was aroused by party feeling, and by political invectives of a considerable portion of the press. It became a popular cry. Had that not occurred, I believe these proceeding would never have arisen.

I solemnly do depreciate the conduct of those who abused the freedom of the press – who have made the proceedings of the Court of Justice the ground on which to prefer a charge against the Government – who, for the sake of political and party motives, have invoked for a second time the criminal judicature of the country."[118]

The Solicitor-General had no direct proof, and the evidence had failed to show that either of the prisoners were aware that Mr Green would proceed on his journey at a certain time with gold. All that Armstrong knew was that Mr Green was going to balance unsettled accounts at Dickens' store.

It was further conceded that Constable Greene knew both prisoners, but could not distinguish them as the murderers. "In fact not one single human being recognises the men,...Constable Greene could never have lost his control...because he can speak of the colour of the man's coat, and other peculiarities of his assailant – and yet he says nothing in the world to point to the identification of those two persons.

Does it not strike you that this is an extraordinary fact, that if one of the prisoners had a horse of his own, and a perfectly distinct one from Davis' horses, if they are the person who committed this robbery and murder – that they should have returned to the scene of their crime in order to steal those horses?

---

118   Argus – July 1,1859

The Second Trial, of Chamberlain and Armstrong.

The witness McMahon says he had known Toke only by dealing with him; and on the 8th January, for the first time, he was asked to come and take care of Toke's store..Toke tells you this is not the first time McMahon had taken charge of the store. Which of the two is telling the truth?

In the former trial McMahon could not remember where Toke was on the 7th yet in this trial he answered: "He was at Gibbo Creek making a road". Taking these circumstances together, and you have a strong proof that McMahon and Toke were acting together for some mysterious purpose.

Certain guns and cartridges and shot are produced – for what purpose beyond a little mala-dramatic effect, I cannot suggest. They do not even correspond in the component parts. I mean the cartridges traced to the prisoner and the slugs with which Green was wounded. If they mean to say that the cartridges fired on the 5th, were of the same description as the shot wound on the 8th, how does it happen that Green's coat was not riddled with shot?

Toke admits that he was transported from England, but would not say for what crime. He also spent a considerable time in several gaols and had been brought to trail for the murder of "Ballaarat Harry". The digger was last seen with Toke, who returned with Ballaarat Harry's horse, dog and a gold nugget. As it was unascertained that Ballaarat Harry was dead the case was dismissed. Unless you believe the evidence of Toke and McMahon there is nothing to effect the prisoners".

The Solicitor- General then rose to his feet and in a clear and polished voice repelled the imputation that he had acted upon the popular cry in again placing the prisoners on trial and claimed that:

"The prisoners have been tried for this crime solely because since the former trial, for the murder of Mr Cornelius Green, additional evidence had been laid before me on so distinct a character as to carry a conviction in my mind of the guilt of the prisoners."

Ireland then rambled on in an attempt to link the facts of the case and finished his address to the jury by stating:

"I strongly recommend the jury to give the prisoners the benefit of any doubt that might be on your minds".

Ten minutes past midnight, after considering for twenty five minutes the jury filed back into the still packed courtroom. The verdict of guilty was received in breathless silence. The effect on the spectators and the witnesses affected one of high emotion. The trial had lasted a meagre day, and upon the outcome two young men, in the prime of the life, stood before the assembled public convicted of the crime of shooting at William Greene, a mounted constable, with intent to murder him on the 5th January 1859.

The amiable Judge Pohlman was then called upon, for the first time in his career, to pass the sentence of death, and he clearly struggled with the emotion which the solemn circumstances of his position gave rise to.

During the unnatural quiet, which prevailed in the packed courtroom, the prisoners were asked if they had anything to say why sentence of death should not be passed upon them?

George Chamberlain, who upon the verdict being pronounced had become flushed in the face, addressed the Court in a firm and determined voice. George said:

"I thank the Judge and the Jury for the patient way in which you have investigated this case, unfortunately however some of the witnesses (and here he turned and stared at me and John McMahon) are guilty of perjury and that it is their evidence solely that has convicted me of this crime alone.

I would ask the gentlemen of the press to convey through their respective newspapers, my thanks to Dr Sewell and Mr Frank Stephen for defending me. They undertook my defence without being asked, and they have acted as friends to mankind through the piece. I would also like to make it known to all of you that I am prepared to meet my Maker with a clear conscience".

William Armstrong, on being asked what he had to say, replied:

"I have nothing to say".

This was typical of Bill, he had never been a talker nor a leader, always the follower and a very minor member of our horse stealing gang.

Judge Pohlman then delivered the final sentence of the law, holding out not the slightest hope of mercy for Chamberlain and Armstrong.

It was half-past twelve before the Court adjourned and it was the last time I saw Armstrong and Chamberlain, they were immediately conveyed to Pentridge Stockade to wait out the time to their executions.[119]

---

119   Mt. Alexander Mail – July 4, 1859.

Armstrong's Confession

Pentridge was yet another stockade to house prisoners in the Colony of Victoria. It was well positioned, being near to Melbourne and yet isolated. The stockade, like the one in Collingwood, was situated in a bluestone area, and so the prisoners could do hard labour breaking up the stones, and in this instance could use the stone for the construction of Sydney Road.

At the time of Chamberlain and Armstrong's imprisonment, the stockade was a typical Pentonville-type prison consisting of single cells with high external bluestone walls with towers for sentries.

The prisoners at Pentridge ate, slept and worked in chains. Prisoners who broke the rules or refused to work were punished by the wearing of heavier irons or were placed in solitary confinement on bread and water.[120]

Armstrong made a full confession to the Reverend Henry Bryan, the chaplain at the Pentridge Stockade. I had no idea of his confession at the time, but I thank God that he did not mention any of the facts that he

---

120 Moreland City Council – History of Moreland Fact Sheet 7 – Pentridge Prison.

raised in his confession at either of the trials. In deference to his loyalty, to this point of time, I will tell you what he said and I can now confirm that he told the truth.

Armstrong explained that he had enlisted as a solider to come out to Victoria, but that he had deserted because he believed he had been punished unnecessarily for minor offences. He had gone to the bush and had lived with a settler for a short while before he went to Omeo. At Omeo, he had lived with me and Ballaarat Harry. Armstrong had confirmed that he had seen Harry's horde of four to five hundred pounds in gold sovereigns and how one evening when we were in our hut alone, I had asked him if he could keep a secret and that I made him swear on my bible that he would do so. I had then asked him to help murder Ballaarat Harry and told him that we would divide Harry's wealth. Armstrong refused to be a party to my plans but promised that he would never say anything about this. True to his word Armstrong did not mention this episode again until days before his death.

In regard to the murder of Cornelius Green, Armstrong claimed that he had tried to fix Green's pistol, and that he could have proved this as Cotty, a resident of Omeo, was there at the time. He did not call Cotty as a witness at either of the trials, as he did not have the means of paying Cotty's expenses to come down from Omeo to give evidence.

On the day before Green's murder, Armstrong stated that he had been on the Omeo Plains and that he had seen me, and that I was searching for Chamberlain. Two hours after that meeting he met up with Chamberlain and asked if he had seen me, he said, "Yes". Armstrong had then returned to his lodgings at Day's hotel.

The following morning Chamberlain has told Billy that he was going to Swift's Creek and as that was on his way he would come with him. After travelling four or five miles on the road, Chamberlain asked Armstrong if he would go with him to stick up Green, as he and some others had made up a plan to do so the day before, and that they were meeting at the race course. Armstrong said he would not be a party to the crime and that he would turn back, but Chamberlain out-smarted him (not a hard thing to do) by saying that he would go with him to the Omeo Plains, as he knew a shortcut back to the route he wished to take.

Needless to say the route taken brought Chamberlain and Armstrong directly to the racecourse, where I was waiting with three guns, one of which was Armstrong's. Armstrong asked me how I had his gun and I told him I had taken it out of his room at the hotel a week before. I also told him that I was glad to have him there, as if I had asked him to join the party he would have refused. Chamberlain and I tried to persuade Armstrong to stick around. I took two straps out of Armstrong's saddle and then we saw Green and his party coming. Armstrong had no time to leave, Green's party were less than one hundred yards away. I then fired three or four shots and Green fell off his horse. Armstrong begged for Green's life, but before he could get off his horse, I had struck Green two or three times with my tomahawk.

I then rounded on Armstrong and asked him where the horse with the gold had gone, he said he neither knew nor cared and then rode away. Chamberlain and I caught up with Armstrong and asked him where he thought he was going. He said that he was going to Livingstone. We told him he was a fool, that he should have gone after the pack horse and that if we were caught we would say that Armstrong was part of the gang.

As usual Billy could not think this problem out and so he went with Chamberlain to a camp site about four miles from my store. The following day I went to the campsite and told Chamberlain that he had better go and get two fresh horses. Armstrong was still intending to return to the diggings, but eventually I persuaded him not to, saying it was too late. I told the boys that as everyone knew that I had been away from the diggings I would go first and see how things were and that I would meet them on the following Saturday.

On the Saturday Chamberlain and Armstrong came to my store, and I told them that they were the only ones suspected of the crime. I convinced Armstrong not to return to the diggings, as he would be locked up for four or five months for nothing.

I then suggested to Chamberlain that he should write to some one on the diggings to say that he was with them at the time of the hold-up and I provided him with the paper to write his alibi. Armstrong never saw what Chamberlain wrote.

Having written a true and accurate report of the crime Armstrong finished his confession by stating:

> "..I have no one to prove my innocence but I saw who did it, and the reason that I never said anything before is that Chamberlain said he should never own to it, for it was all the same to him. He said 'let everyone fight his own battle' and it would serve me right if I was hung for not joining them and getting the gold.

So what must I do – be hanged and let the guilty escape, because I would not join them, but I have never denied having been there, and never will, and may the Lord have mercy on my soul".[121]

Armstrong's confession was forwarded to the Chief Secretary. I have no doubt that Chamberlain also wrote a confession, but obviously, it

---

121   Confession of William Armstrong.

Armstrong's Confession

did not have the impact of the one written by Armstrong. The Chief Secretary returned the papers including Armstrong's confession to the Reverend Bryan under cover of a letter in which he said that he had read "most of the documents you have submitted me..I do not meet with anything in Chamberlains statement which can, conclusively, taken as a whole, disparate Armstrong's statement, on the contrary it confirmed many important facts...Nothing that I have read tends to remove the impression that Toke himself is one of the persons who committed the deeds – His statements unravel his character...I cannot resist the impression that Toke was an accomplice – if not the real instigator – confirmed by Armstrong's statement..."[122]

For his final words in respect of Armstrong's fate Reverend Bryan wrote: "I shall be with (Armstrong) on Monday, the day previous to the execution but shall not refer to the past unless he expressly wishes to give any further statement. I have advised him to devote the few remaining days to penitential exercise".[123]

Lucky for me that it was generally believed (with the exception of Dr Sewell and the Reverend Bryan) that Armstrong had implicated me in his confession hoping that I would be arrested and tried, and subsequently his execution would be delayed so that he could be a witness at my trial. It was also believed that my implication in the murder might have been concocted between Chamberlain and Armstrong whilst they were in the Pentridge Stockade.[124]

George Chamberlain and William Armstrong, both aged twenty-three, were executed on the 12th July 1859. Chamberlain died quickly because of his size and weight, but Armstrong's death was slow and tortuous.

---

122 Correspondence dated Pentridge 8th July 1859.
123 Correspondence relating to R-v- Chamberlain and Armstrong.
124 Mt.Alexander Mail – July 11 1859.

Armonstrong's death certificate

Chamberlain's death certificate

They were buried in the Melbourne Cemetery in unmarked graves, no one mourned their deaths and no one gained by their demise.

Casts of Armstrong, Chamberlain and Trooper Greene were to be seen at Madame Lee's Waxworks at 97 Bourke Street Melbourne for some time after the trial.[125]

---

125 Bushranging Omeo Road, newspaper clipping from unknown paper.

The Aftermath

Despite the Victorian Government's drastic steps in re-trying Armstrong and Chamberlain, their executions were not enough to return popular support to the O'Shanassy Ministry.

The Constitutional Associations' political propaganda had worked. The government was crushed and was left with only a dozen supporters. Four ministers (including Ireland) were defeated in Melbourne at the following elections.

The majority of the witnesses, including myself returned to Omeo, which by this stage was now a fully-fledged town with a population of six hundred diggers. A cairn to the memory of Cornelius Green was promptly erected at Swift's Creek, the site of his murder.

Constable Green was given a year's pay by the Police Commissioner and was discharged, as unfit, from the force. He did not return to Omeo, immigrating to New Zealand where I am told he joined their police force and was an active member for forty years.

There was another reason for the Chief of Police to do some investigation into the handling of the case by his officers in Livingstone. Robert James Fisher, a student of medicine, had inspected Cornelius Green's body and gave evidence at the initial inquest into Green's death. "For visiting the body of the late Mr Green at Tongio" Fisher was paid two pounds despite Inspector Hill knowing that Fisher was not a legally qualified practitioner. Fisher was, therefore precluded by law from payment for giving evidence at the magistrate's inquiry. Fisher was paid for this and his attendances and operations on the luckless Constable Greene. Inquiries into Fisher's qualifications and treatment of William Greene had begun as early as April 1859 when the Chief Medical Officer in Melbourne had requested a detailed report of Greene's injuries and confirmation of Fisher's qualifications. Inspector Hill had replied in a written memo that Fisher had made upwards of twenty visits to Constable Greene from the 5th January to the 25th February and that he had removed slugs from both arms, two from one arm lying on the shaft of the humerus and two others from the other arm that were in close connection with the ulnar nerve. Inspector Hill concluded by saying that Mr Fisher had stated that he held credentials for a complete course of study of Medicine of Surgery, the last two years of which were from Queens College Galway and the previous from the Principal Medical Schools at Dublin.[126]

The fact of the matter was that there was no qualified doctor residing in the vicinity of Omeo and therefore Robert Fisher had been called in to render his services to the injured trooper. In total he had received the sum of one hundred and forty- nine pounds, which he was not legally entitled to and rather than suffer the humiliation of being forced to repay the sum, he donated the money to William Greene. Quite a clever little ploy as it gave the good "doctor" a humane reputation. He also

---

[126] Memo from Inspector Hill, Livingstone Creek 13 April 1859.

The Aftermath

knew the government would never attempt to recover the money from the incapacitated trooper. I had a good laugh about Fisher's misfortune. After all, he was the one who had laid an official complaint against me regarding the disappearance of Ballaarat Harry. Now his reputation and standing within the community was in tatters.

The penny-pinching Paymaster of Police in Melbourne then began to examine the costs in respect of the conveyance of James Mc Mahon by coach from Back Creek to Melbourne to give evidence in the second trial of Chamberlain and Armstrong. The Court had made an allowance to McMahon, and the government refused to reimburse further costs incurred by McMahon. It appeared that Cobb & Co. had charged McMahon five shillings more than his allowance, it was made patently clear in numerous memos that Inspector Hill of the Livingstone Police Station would have to make up the difference himself!

Hill was also queried about the travelling costs of Constable White, who had travelled to Back Creek to deliver the subpoena to McMahon, and to accompany him to Melbourne by coach. Hill was forced to write a number of memos confirming that Constable White did not proceed to or return from Back Creek under a subpoena of the Supreme Court, but as a Constable travelling on ordinary police duty (in search of McMahon) and therefore did not received any allowance whatever for the duty. White's account for two pounds ten shillings, for his coach ride, was I believe eventually paid.

It was certainly not all beer and skittles for Inspector Hill who was responsible for rendering all accounts in respect of the running of the Livingstone Police District to his superiors in Melbourne. Inspector Hill had, it appeared, made two serious errors in accounts forwarded to Melbourne for payment. The Chief Commissioner of Police, Frederick

Standish roundly admonished Hill and wrote " I had scarcely written my minute to Mr Hill respecting the overcharges in McLeod's (account), when Marshall's claim was rendered, including the item of 1000lb of oats delivered on 5th March, (and) for which an (account) was passed in May last on Mr Hill's Certificate. The duplicate receipts both also signed by Mr Hill are attached.

I regret extremely to have to notice so serious an oversight, the amount involved £81-6/3- is large, (and) the error being the second of this kind, it tends of course to shake the high opinion I entertained of Mr Hill's business qualities."[127]

As always Inspector Hill had a defence and wrote back to the Chief Commissioner saying "I beg to state that the day after the Post left I discovered the error in Marshall's (account) and forwarded the Paymaster a corrected Voucher for the same – I regret exceedingly that I should have committed such a mistake which was mainly caused by my having to hurry away an arrear of correspondence which I found here on my return from Melbourne – otherwise I should have observed that I had already sent in a voucher for this".[128]

I find it bloody amazing that Hill can make such mistakes and receive nothing more than a harsh memo from his boss. If I had made such an error I would have found myself in gaol!

With so much paperwork being shuffled between Hill's superiors and the Inspector it was a wonder how the Police at Livingstone Station ever did any police work, but occasionally they reported to their superiors information that did not involve accounts. In correspondence to the Chief Commissioner of Police, Inspector Hill reported on the 26th July

---

127 Memo from Chief Commissioner of Police, F Standish 8 August 1859.
128 Memo from Inspector Hill Livingstone Creek 30 August 1859

1859 that the horse stealing gang had disbanded. Hill was anxious to show that the trial of Chamberlain and Armstrong had had an effect in his district. He explained to his superior that he had long suspected certain individuals as being connected with the horse stealing gang, and that the gang members had anticipated revelations being made by Chamberlain and Armstrong, which would implicate them, and hence gang members were anxious to leave the district where they were so well known.

Hill correctly guessed that the individuals would all travel to New South Wales as they had confederates there who had in the past assisted in disposing of horses. Sidney Penny had on his release from gaol immediately taken himself off to Wagga Wagga in New South Wales. In late July of 1859 a Frenchman in the vicinity of Beechworth had met Jack Sheean and Clarke, on their way to the Murray River, which is the border between New South Wales and Victoria. They had threatened the fellow with future violence if he reported their meeting.

The Frenchy immediately reported his rendezvous with the two horsemen to the Police, which prompted Inspector Hill to request that the Commissioner of Police send a telegraphic message along the line in the direction of Sydney, which might intercept Jack Sheean and Clarke who, would almost certainly have stolen horses in their possession as they had none of their own when last seen in the district.

Hill finalised his report to the Commissioner of Police in Melbourne by stating " I should feel much assisted in my endeavours to clear up this affair, if I were put in possession of any information which may have been communicated by the prisoners Chamberlain and Armstrong previous to their death, and touching upon the operations of this notorious gang

– should such be conveyed to me I of course would strictly use it for Police purposes".[129]

Hill did not receive a reply from Melbourne and remained sublimely ignorant of the content of Armstrong's confession.

I had long since decided to call the Gibbo my home and was content to returned to my store in its secluded location. It would not have been possible for me to move to New South Wales or Tasmania. With my past convictions in both colonies I would have been noticed immediately. Police in neighbouring colonies were well aware of my recent activities. I was a marked man.

The gang had reduced dramatically in number but I did not lack for company, I had my pack of dogs and a reputation I was proud of. I had enhanced my appearance by wearing a hat made of platypus skins and with a broken nose and a misshapen arm, which also had been broken in a fracas, my appearance was truly menacing. I was pleased to be left to my own devises.

The people of Omeo wished to shed their reputation as a rough and ready gold-mining town and even gave a testimonial to Mr Thomas Sheean, to honour him as a pillar of respectability and a civic-minded gentleman. The testimonial, which was observed by a general holiday by the miners, occurred on the 24th September 1859. It also happened to be the first field day of the Omeo Cricket Club, which had been established under the Presidency of the one and only resident Magistrate, Mr. Wills. The presentation of the testimonial, which consisted of a silver-mounted saddle and bridle, and their equipment, was entrusted to Mr John Wright, the late member at the Mining Board.

---

129 Letter to Chief Commissioner of Police from Inspector Hill 26 July 1859.

The Aftermath

Addressing Mr Sheean, John Wright said "It has long been felt by my brother miners and myself, that a public acknowledgment was due to you for the aid you have rendered in opening up this gold field, and giving assistance where required to such miners as possessed the necessary energy, but not the requisite capital to develop its hidden wealth. A further tribute is due for the personal risk you have run in aiding the public authorities in tracking notorious offenders against law and order, through the wild bush in a district so little known as Omeo, except to old bushmen like yourself. On your social qualities, I need not dwell in the presence of those around me who know you as well as I do, but for all those reasons I have much pleasure in presenting you with this proof, slight that it may be, yet heartily given of how much you are appreciated by those among whom your lot has been cast, and of sincerely wishing you in their name a long life of happiness and prosperity".

Mr Sheean replied " I thank you Sir, and all friends for the kindness you have displayed in presenting me with this testimonial of your esteem; to gain the good will of all around me has been my great aim, and the proceedings of this evening assure me that I have not laboured in vain. Again gentlemen, I thank you heartily and sincerely".

The speech making was getting rather long-winded by that stage, but Police Magistrate Wills was not to be outdone, as a man used to addressing a captive audience he stated that "it was pleasing to him, although simply attending the present meeting as one of the subscribers to the Sheean testimonial, that an opportunity should thus be afforded him of publicly expressing his thanks to those of his respected friend. Mr Inspector Hill, who was also a subscriber, was on duty in Gipps Land, but he too had made it clear that he thought Mr Sheean had been an invaluable aid to the authorities of Omeo, on three occasions and at considerable expense and risk to himself".

Three cheers were then given for Mr Sheean, and it was then that I noticed Soames Davis at my side. Soames whispered to me, that he knew a way in which he too could obtain such a testimonial. Fool, with those words he signed his own death warrant, although I would take my time in executing it. I had thought that my menacing looks and my violent reputation would have been enough to stop anyone from threatening me. Obviously Soames did not think that I would dare to raise a hand against another resident in the district. I would certainly make him regret that he had ever challenged me.

The subscribers to the testimonial adjourned to a public supper and ball at Mr Sheean's house, and the dancing I am told was kept up with much spirit till a late hour.[130]

I of course did not attend the ball, nor did my remaining mate John Paynter .We would not have been made welcome. When I returned to my store I was content to resume my previous life-style and to formulate a plan to deal with the loathsome Soames Davis. John, who had been acquitted of the charge of accessory after the fact in Armstrong and Chamberlain's first trial, took his time to wind up his business as a butcher, in Omeo. He had again come under the scrutiny of the local police.

The Police Gazette of the 3rd November 1859 carried the following information: " A Warrant for the arrest of John Payne, alias Paynter, has been issued at Beechworth in which he is charged with stealing a brown filly, the property of Robert Gregory, Allen's Flat, Yackandandah, on 15th September last. Description of Payne, aged about 30 years, 6 ft. high, fresh complexion, dark hair, rather thin on top of head, a large aquiline

---

130   Gippsland Guardian – 9 September 1859 – Omeo Weekly Summary.

nose. The filly was seen in Payne's possession on the road to Omeo with JC newly branded on near shoulder"[131]

Paynter, was arrested in Omeo on the 15th November 1859, Inspector Hill was fairly glowing when he wrote, in his dispatch to Melbourne:

> "John Payne alias Paynter charged with horse stealing at Yackandanda in September, last was this day apprehended here and remanded to Beechworth to be further dealt with. Stolen horse has not been recovered and has probably been disposed of by him at Snowy Creek or some other place on the Omeo route as he did not make his appearance here with the animal".

On the 7th December 1859 Paynter faced the Beechworth Court but as the prosecution was not able to produce either the witness or the horse, the Magistrate dismissed the charge.[132]

Paynter packed up his family and like his brother-in-law, Sidney Penny, moved to Wagga Wagga in New South Wales.

By the start of 1860, the horse-stealing gang had been re-located to New South Wales. I kept in contact with the gang members. We knew every track and by-way from Omeo to Wagga Wagga. We could travel the by-ways with immunity, as we had many a willing hand to shelter us in return for a small payment, or the opportunity to purchase a horse at a good price. Constable Fane, who was attached to the police station at Livingstone, had once been assigned to follow Paytner. The luckless policeman followed Paynter for over a month from Omeo, across the Gibbo Creek, Wheelers River to Albury, Table Top and Wagga Wagga and back via the Mitta Mitta River, a total of seven hundred miles. Fane

---

131 Police Gazette No.26 – November 1859
132 Cattlemen and Huts of the High Plains – Harry Stephenson

never obtained one scrap of information that would lead to the identity or arrest of a gang member.[133] Paynter was such a consummate bushman that he was able to lead the Constable on a wild-goose chase without the police officer ever suspecting that he was thus being used. Mind you most of us were capable of such a rouse; and I for one was also able to trek long distances on foot. On many occasion I walked across Mt Hotham to Beechworth or Yackandandah even in the midst of winter in the snow.

As I have said, it was necessary for me to keep out of the way of the authorities for some time. This was not too hard to do, as my store was some thirty miles from the township of Omeo, and the police were always short of horses or officers, so they rarely called on me. In fact Inspector Hill was instructed to turn his attention to the plans for the police reserves in the Omeo District, these plans were to include police buildings at the Mitchell River and Bruthen.

Hill was experiencing real difficulties at Livingstone Creek where a reserve had been set out by Mr Assistant Surveyor Pettit to include a proposed new court of Petty Sessions. The police paddock had been fenced in but had not been proclaimed a reserve. Hill was entreating his superiors yet again in Melbourne, to do so immediately, as miners continued to work on the site.[134] The Police kept their horses in the paddock and as their horses were not on a par with the livestock owned by locals, they had no desire for their broken down nags to be further threatened by pot holes left by the miners. Of a more serious threat was also the fact that recovered livestock was also penned up in the paddock. There was usually a period of time before the rightful owner could retrieve his animal, as it was often held as evidence in a trial, and the

---

133 Police Correspondence – 12 October 1858.
134 Memo Inspector Hill – 31 August 1859

police could not afford for the animal to be damaged or lost whilst in their possession.

The good old days had passed and there was yet another influx of miners to the diggings. There was the Frenchman Louis Lafeber and the Chinese with their strange names like Ah Cheong, Ah Keong Ah Yow and Ah Chun. New diggers, were not familiar with my mode of operations, this suited me fine. I was able to exploit their gullibility by selling them goods at inflated prices at my store and I was also able to go about my business unmolested, as they had no knowledge of my past misdemeanours.

Pay Back Time

Many activities came to a stand still during the winter months in the Omeo District. The extreme conditions prevented much travel. It was also not practical to transport quantities of gold to places like Beechworth or to Gipps Land, as the heavily laden pack animals could not negotiate the snow-covered or at best wet and boggy tracks from May until August each year.

In 1862 spring came early and by the 5th August, the weather was good enough for Soames Davis to set off from Henry Lee's house at Lee's Punt on the Little River with a quantity of gold, his destination was to be Yackandandah. Although the destinations differed Soames proposed trip was strikingly similar to the one taken by that of the late Cornelius Green.

Soames Davis, the former partner of Cornelius Green, departed Lee's house riding one horse and leading another. On an isolated patch of ground close to the Yackandandah Creek I had concealed myself and waited for my quarry. Soames was so confident in his own capabilities that he was travelling alone. As Soames approached my concealed position I called out to him, "Remember Cornelius Green?" That stopped him dead in his tracks and he answered in a shaky voice "Who are you and what do you want?" I replied, "Soames Davis I want your gold and your life!".

I did not give Soames the opportunity to raise his gun, I was still a strong man and was above average height, five feet seven inches in fact, I leaped forward and dragged Soames from his horse before he knew what was happening. Soames lay stunned on the ground with me standing over him. With my trusty tomahawk in hand, I allowed him just enough time to realise who I was and what I was about to do, before I despatched him in just the same way as I had done to his partner nigh on three years before.

After the deed was done, I stripped Soames body and buried it at a spot that no one would locate. I concealed his clothes in different places and departed the scene with the late Mr Soames Davis' precious watch and gold. I did not bother about his horse, as it was too much of a risk to attempt to dispose of such a well-known animal.

The talk of the diggings became the disappearance of Soames Davis, as on the very day that he disappeared, in fact at 3.00pm his horse was found loose in the bush. A search party was arranged and subsequently Davis' coat was found planted under branches of trees about one hundred yards from Yackandandah Creek, close to the crossing. Half a mile further on his boots and trousers were found, also planted and near the creek sticks were found with human hair adhering to them, whilst footprints were found leading into the water. Spots of blood were found on Soames' saddle as well as spur marks, as if the rider had been violently pulled off his horse. The search party concluded the Soames Davis had been murdered and his body concealed.[135]

---

135   Victoria Police Gazette – 4 September 1862

The people of the district of Omeo were none to pleased to receive the news that another gold agent had been murdered. Thomas Easton, of Livingstone Creek, another pillar of respectability, immediately offered fifty pounds for the conviction of the murderer. There was no interest in the reward and the offer was again noted a month later in the Victoria Police Gazette.[136]

If only the death and attempted robbery of Cornelius Green had been so brilliantly executed. If Armstrong and Chamberlain had my guile and temperament they too may have walked free. Although I am sure some of the older residents of Livingstone Creek must have noted the similarities of the murders, no one even if they thought it, dared to challenge me about the matter. Naturally I had ensured that I had a watertight alibi, and as gold dust could not be easily identified, and I had disposed of Davis' highly prized gold open-faced watch, there was no evidence to incriminate me.

At last I could lay the death of Cornelius Green to rest. Armstrong, Chamberlain and now Soames Davis were all dead. Miss Mutter was back in the old country and Trooper Greene was off fighting crime in New Zealand. Henry Dickens and John McMahon had both the common sense to take leave of the immediate area, and of course Sidney Penny and John Paytner were residing in Wagga Wagga in the Colony of New South Wales.

Soames Davis' death did not even cause a ripple of concern. His death was not even mentioned in the influential newspapers of the Colony. Davis' whole being was soon forgotten and within months of his disappearance you would have been hard pushed to find a digger at Livingstone Creek who knew of the man.

---

136 Victoria Police Gazette – 16 October 1862.

So you see, you can commit the perfect crime. I regained my security and improved my finances on the 5th August 1862 and got away with the crime scot-free!

1863

In 1863 the last of the survivors of the Cornleius Green party departed the Livingstone Creek area. Harry (the Snob) Dickens had always imagined that he was superior to the rest of the people who inhabited the Livingstone, he had no intentions of living out his days in that backwater. Dickens' made his plans and eventually purchased the Criterion Hotel in Sale. The hotel was a two-storey brick building complete with wrought iron balustrades. Dickens moved up in the world and out of my reach.

And so I settled back into my familiar life style. I ran my store, grew some fruit and vegetables and 'cared' for the odd horse that came my way. I found it necessary to hire some help, as I was now in my fifty-second year and the hard life that I had lead was starting to take its toll on my body.

It was not difficult to employ someone, although still remote, the Omeo District had its fair share of failed miners, who for a variety of reasons could not or would not return to their previous calling. I of course had to be extremely prudent in whom I chose to employ, and if I am totally honest with you, there were some who chose not to be closely associated with the likes of me. I required a hard worker, but I also needed a gullible employee who took orders without question. It was a shame that poor

Billy the Groom was no longer alive, with his gift with animals, and his trusting nature, he would have been perfect for the job. Alas he had been gone for four years and so I looked around for some time before I located Adam Loftus Lynn.

With Lynn, a failed miner, ensconced at the Gibbo I could turn my attention to legitimate business. It was time again for me to seek justice through the Courts, and so the Court of Petty Sessions at Omeo opened with a flurry of business in 1863. On the 6th January 1863 I was the plaintiff in a total of three cases involving debts owed to me for goods supplied. John Buckley owed me twelve pounds, sixteen shillings and nine and a half pence, John Turner owed thirteen pounds, thirteen shillings and nine pence and David Brown owed nineteen pounds, nine shillings and sixpence. These new bucks thought that they could take advantage of an old man. Well they had another thing coming. I had the law on my side and was more than happy to recover outstanding debts in this way. Of course if Buckley, Turner and Brown did not pay up I could always resort to other methods of persuasion.

I was again forced to resort to court action in February 1863 when I sued David Brown for a further sum of twelve pounds, fourteen shillings and six pence and Richard Henessy for the sum of nine pounds and nine shillings. As John Buckley had not paid his debt in accordance with an order of the court made in January, a Warrant of Distress was issued against him.

Unfortunately before I could recover all my debts I was once again the subject of a further charge for horse stealing. Sergeant King, who was stationed at the Livingstone Creek Police Station, had charged Adam Loftus Lynn and me with horse stealing. Our first court appearance was on the 26th February 1863. We were both remanded. I might add that we were both remanded a total of six times. On our seventh appearance, on the 2nd April I was discharged, and Lynn was committed to stand trial at the next Circuit Court in Beechworth on Saturday the 11th April 1863.[137]

I was a very relieved man when I walked out of the Court that day, but I had a gut feeling that I had not heard the last of this matter. I did not believe that Lynn would have the ability to talk his way out of a prison sentence. I was however wondering what I had done to have yet another incompetent employee, who had the potential, if he told the truth, to land me in trouble with the law.

When Lynn arrived in Beechworth he gave a full statement to the Police, and shortly after he began describing himself as my servant, and that all of his actions taken in respect of the horses in question was on my instructions. Adam Lynn would not have had the intelligent or the legal expertise to know what a servant/master relationship was and the connotations of this relationship in the eyes of the law. Of course it was the police who wised him up to this. Lynn was offered the intelligence of being discharged if he would give evidence against me, if I were charged with horse stealing. The Police at Livingstone Station had been out to get me for a long time and now they had their puppet!

My cronies knew that I was up to my neck in the horse-stealing racket, but so were they and so they would not give me away; however one loose remark made by John Turner, started the ball rolling. John had seen me riding the stolen mare in question and had boasted about this when he was in his cups one night. Unfortunately, the remark was passed on to Senior Constable Pepper of the Snowy Creek Police Station. Pepper was

---

137 Omeo Petty Sessions Record Book.

fully acquainted with the facts of the case, and began to make further inquiries.

Once satisfied that there was a case to answer Senior Constable James Pepper, Officer in Charge of Police at Snowy Creek obtained a Warrant for my arrest. I was arrested on the 9th August 1863. The charge was stated as:

> "at the Water Holes near Omeo did feloniously steal take and lead ride or drove away one Brown mare branded NRB off shoulder the property of one Charles H Hodgson of Omeo".

Omeo had built its first gaol in 1858, it was like many other of the buildings in and around the area and was simply a log cabin. Until this time I had not sampled the accommodation. It was a most unpleasant experience for an old man in August, without a fire it was a very chilling experience.

Nothing better than a scenic route to a trial. My initial appearance was at Yackandandah on the 22nd of August 1863 before Justices of the Peace, Welshman and Lane. When the charge was read to me I stated:

> "I leave it entirely to yourselves"[138]

Subpoenas to give evidence were then issued for James Pepper, Charles Howell Hodgson, Adam Loftus Lynn and Joseph Pedrazzi.

I was then off to stand trial at the District Circuit Court at Beechworth on the 21st October 1863.

I had made numerous trips to Beechworth but this was the first time I had travelled under police guard. Beechworth was of course another

---

[138] Statement of the Accused, Thomas Toke.

town that owed its origins to gold. Situated on a granite barren ridge it had a population of somewhere between thirty and forty thousand by the late 1850's. By 1858 there was a resident County Court Judge, Thomas Cope, four barristers, several solicitors, at least six doctors and four banks, the Oriental, Victoria, New South Wales and Australasia.[139] Beechworth boasted a hospital for the aged, gaol and a general hospital. The gaol, far more impressive than it counterpart in Omeo consisted of a number of wooden buildings surrounded by a stockade, it had been completed towards the end of 1853.

The Law Courts at Beechworth were opened in 1855, which was a very auspicious year for the town, as it was in that year also that Robert O'Hara Burke, later to be a famous explorer, arrived in Beechworth. In 1856 Beechworth was declared a District, the town's roads and footpaths were formalised and the Council prohibited the erection of canvas-built shops or homes. Beechworth also became the major administrative centre for the whole of northeast Victoria and Police, Petty Sessions, Mining Board, County and Supreme Court hearings all took place in the town.[140]

Enough of Beechworth, if you are so interested in the town, go visit it yourselves! I for one would have been more than pleased to forgo the pleasure in September of 1863. Instead I was back in court and you know by now that the first thing I enquire about is who was the presiding judge. I knew I was done for as soon as I was informed that I would be appearing before His Honour Redmond Barry. Barry had a fine mind and no doubt he would remember that he had been my Counsel in 1841 when I was convicted of horse stealing. Redmond Barry had of course come up in the world since then. In 1842 he had been appointed a commissioner of

---

139 Recollections of a Victorian Police Officer – John Sadleir
140 Beechworth – www.beechworth-index.com.au

the Court of Requests, at a salary of one hundred pounds per year. He was also well known for his interest in the cultural life of the community and allowed people interested in literature to use his library at his house in Bourke Street, Melbourne. He was one of the founders and the first president of the Mechanics' Institute, afterwards the Athenaeum Library. He was also one of the founders of the Melbourne Hospital and in January 1852 became a judge of the Supreme Court of Victoria, all this by the age of thirty-eight years![141]

The exalted Judge Barry was to preside over the Crown -v- Thomas Toke. A case which was instigated on the 19th February, at 10.00pm to be precise, by Mr Frederick Braithwait attending the Livingstone Creek Police Station. Braithwait, the overseer for Mr DeGraves at the Omeo Station, reported to Sergeant King that on that morning he had noticed where a mob of horses had been rounded up and that he had tracked them to the Gibbo Road. On the morning of the 20th February Sgt. King and Constable Gilligan went to the Plains and followed the tracks of the horses to Jack Sheeans' stockyard. The Police maintained that the horses had been kept at the stockyard for a short time and then had been moved on. Constable Gilligan was supposed to have tracked the horses for a further three days until he lost their tracks at the foot of the Gibbo where it runs down to the river Mitta Mitta opposite Italian Point.

Sgt King then resumed the search for the mob of horses and alleged that they must have remained at Italian Point for some time. He therefore went to Joseph Pedrazzi's hut, which was about a hundred yards from the Point. Joseph informed King that he and his mates had seen a mob of nine or ten horses on the Point on the evening of the 20th February. Joseph also claimed that he had seen a brown mare, running lose and that it was branded on the off shoulder with the letters NRB. The mare

---

141 Dictionary of Australian Biography

had a saddle and bridle on and a white coat was strapped to the saddle. The Italian stated that the saddle and bridle belonged to me and that, shortly after he had noticed the mare, Adam Lynn arrived riding a bay mare branded with a heart on the off shoulder and claimed that the brown mare belonged to a man that was at my place. Lynn, the Italian said, maintained that the mare had broken away from him.

On the 25th February at 6.00am Sgt King arrived at my hut asking very awkward questions. He asked me about the brown mare and I told him that I had given it back to her owner, and that I could not remember the owner's name or address. I also denied any knowledge of the horse, branded with a heart, which Lynn had been riding. I had not had time to think of answers or to obtain an alibi, because Lynn, the bloody foul had not told me that he had been seen riding the 'heart' mare or that he had a conversation with anyone about the brown mare.

Sgt King then asked Lynn the same questions regarding the two horses, and in my presence, Lynn wisely denied any knowledge of the animals. Sergeant King did not find any trace of the mares on my property. I knew my business, the mob of horses had long gone, they were well on their way to New South Wales, where they would be sold for high prices.

On the 1st March both the 'heart' mare and the brown mare were located at Italian Point. Sgt King arrived the following day and found that the brown mare was in hobbles in the Mitta Mitta River and the 'heart' mare by the bank. The Sergeant left the brown mare with Joseph Pedrazzi and returned to Omeo with the 'heart' mare.

John Hodgson, claimed the brown mare. On returning to Wombat, from Snowy Creek, Hodgson stopped at Pedrazzi's and claimed that the mare was the property of Charles Hodgson, his brother.

As no one had actually seen me with any of the horses, the initial charge brought against me by Sergeant King had been discharged. Lynn of course, had never had any dealings with the law before and once in Beechworth Gaol, had decided that he would confess.

Adam Loftus Lynn stated, in his confession and in evidence at my trial, that he was a miner and that he had been in my employment in February 1863. On the 17th February he saw the 'heart' mare at the Water Hole, about four miles from my home. Lynn claimed that he went with me to that place on my orders. That I had told Lynn that I was going for some horses I had brought from a man called Worster and that Lynn was there to help me drive the horses. Not content to dob me in he also confirmed that John Dudley Jones was present at the time and that he had accompanied us as far as the top of the Gib before he turned back.

Lynn went on to say that we had rounded up a mob of fourteen horses on the Omeo Plains and with the other ten from Italian Point, were put into the yard. He claimed that I was riding the brown mare, and that I had placed my own saddle and bridle on her and that I rode her away in the direction of Jones' place. Lynn stated that he had never seen the brown mare before that day and that he was riding a horse that I had given him.

In order to round the horses up at Italian Point, Lynn stated that I got off the brown mare and began to throw stones at the horses. The mare, still saddled followed the horses across the river and that on my instructions, he was sent to try and find her. If any one challenged him, Lynn, claimed that I told him to say that the mare belonged to a man at my place. Lynn then put me right in it by stating that there was no man at my place and that I never said to whom the animal belonged. After retrieving the horse from Italian Point Lynn further claimed that he had brought the mare to me, and that I had hobbled her and turned her down the river.[142]

At my trial Joseph Pedrazzi, a miner, stated that in February 1863 he had been living at Italian Point and that he had known me for two years and that he also knew Adam Lynn. At about 2 o'clock on the 20th of February, he had seen a mob of strange horses. Amongst the horses he noted one with a saddle and a bridle, and he went down to investigate. He said that he and his mate took the saddle and the bridle off the mare and that he knew they were mine as I had lent them to him on occasions. (Do a good turn and see what happens? You get betrayed.)

Pedrazzi continued his evidence, stating that Lynn had come to him and asked for the saddle, bridle and the brown mare. He had then given them to Lynn and had not seen the saddle since that day.[143]

Charles Howell Hodgson gave evidence. He swore that he was a clerk and resident of Omeo and that the mare branded NRB was his property. He had purchased the horse in Omeo in June 1862, she was valued at ten pounds and he had never known her to stray. Hodgson confirmed that he only knew me by sight and I had never sold him any horses. He finished his evidence by stating that he had not sold the mare or authorised anyone else to do so.[144]

Senior Constable Pepper was the last of the prosecution witnesses. He stated that John Turner, who lived at Station Point, Mitta Mitta, had admitted to several people that he had seen me riding the brown mare. Pepper conceded that when he had asked Turner about his statement, he refused to admit that he had said anything. Pepper was allowed to

---

142 Adam Loftus Lynn's confession.
143 Joseph Pedrazzi's sworn statement dated 22 August 1863.
144 Charles Howell Hodgson's sworn statement dated 22 August 1863.

continue his hearsay evidence and stated that just before I was arrested Turner had remarked to me " You got out of that scrape well at Omeo" and I was reported to laugh and reply, "Oh I had nothing to do with it but I know who did do it". Senior Constable Pepper clarified this by saying that we were referring to the mob of horses and not the brown mare.

I wonder what Joseph Pedrazzi would say about him giving evidence, if he knew what Pepper had reported to his superiors. Pepper had said that Turner "would be a great deal better witness than Pedrazzi" because he was English.[145]

Mr C.A.Smyth Crown Prosecutor had done his job. My Counsel, Mr Stephen and my attorney Mr Young, did all that they could, but it would not have mattered what they had said in my defence. I was done for.

On the 22 October 1863 I was found guilty of horse stealing and sentenced to seven years on the roads with hard labour.[146] Initially I was taken to the Beechworth Gaol and from there to Pentridge in Melbourne on the 1st December 1863.

I have already described Pentridge Prison to you, it had not altered since the incarceration of Chamberlain and Armstrong some four years before.

Officially I was to be known as prisoner number 6784 and again my description was carefully noted. By 1863 my aged was recorded as fifty-five. My hair had begun to grey and although I had suffered a broken nose and arm since I had left the old country, I was still a healthy looking specimen. I stood at five feet seven inches, which meant that I had grown a full ten inches since the time of my transportation. I was described as

---

145 Letter written by Senior Constable Pepper dated 22 September 1863.
146 Queen –v- Toke for Horse Stealing.

possessing an oval face with a fresh complexion, gone was the sallow and pox pitted face of my youth. My tattoos and moles were mentioned and it was duly recorded that I could both read and write. What would have Chamberlain and Armstrong said about that?

Although I would never be described as a model prisoner, I was now considered old and found myself surrounded by stronger and younger prisoners. I still had my reputation and my guile, and it was this that would see me through yet another sentence.

The main gate of HM Prison Beechworth

The Tichborne Case

It is necessary for me now to digress to explain the background of the famous Tichborne Case. Bear with me, and I will explain my relevance to this unsolved and perplexing mystery.

Roger Charles Tichborne was born in 1829 into a titled and extremely wealth family. Roger's uncle was the eighth baronet of Tichborne. Roger's mother was Henriette Felicite, an illegitimate child of an English Seymour and a French Bourbon Conti. Henriette detested her husband and loathed the Tichborne family, she spent most of her time in Paris. Roger was a victim of his parent's bitter arguments, they fought over his education and with whom he should reside. Up to a point Henriette won, but in 1845 Roger was sent to England to finish his schooling at Stonyhurst.

In 1845 the eighth baronet died and was succeed by his brother, who had no children. This effectively meant that Roger's father was the heir to the baronetcy.

After leaving Stonyhurst Roger took a junior commission with the 6th Dragoon Guards in 1849, served in Ireland until 1852 and briefly in Canterbury before he resigned his commission.

Roger was known for his fondness for liquor, a desire to see the world and an extremely moody disposition. His family rejected his choice of a bride and in a fit of pique, in March 1853, sailed from Le Harve for Valparaiso in South America. For ten months he travelled through South American, however by then he had began to drink heavily and had run out of money.

On the 20 April 1854 Roger left Kingston on board the ship "Bella". The ship disappeared, evidently with the loss of all on board.

In March 1853 Roger's father became the tenth baron of Tichborne, and although his wife had been elevated to the title Lady Tichborne, she continued to quarrel with her husband and his family. When told that Roger had drowned at sea, Lady Tichborne refused to believe that this was so. Lady Tichborne's relationship with her husband did not improve and when her husband died in June 1862, the baronetcy passed to Roger's younger brother Alfred.

Lady Tichborne (Nataional Portrait Gallery)

If possible, Alfred was a worse character than his elder brother and was remarkably profligate. His mother, now Dowager, still believed that Roger was alive and she therefore began to search for him in the hope that he would return and take his rightful title, Earl of Tichborne.[147]

The Dowager placed advertisements throughout the world's press in expectation of contacting her son. Advertisements were even placed in newspapers in the colonies because it was rumoured that some survivors of the "Bella" had been rescued by American whalers and put to shore at their next destination, being Tasmania.

In August 1865 an advertisement appeared in colonial newspapers seeking information about the fate of Tichborne. Mr William Gibbes, a solicitor in Wagga Wagga New South Wales, responded to the advertisement claiming that George Orton was the missing heir.

Despite some glaring discrepancies Orton was able to advance his claim and leaving Sydney in September 1866 travelled to Paris, where the Dowager recognised him and proclaimed him as her missing son. This was despite the fact that Orton was obese (Roger had been extremely thin) spoke vulgar English, and could not understand a word of French, which was basically Tichborne's native language. The Dowager handed Orton Tichborne's papers and many family letters, and also gave him a yearly allowance of one thousand pounds. Orton proceeded to England and began investigating details in respect of the Tichborne home, visited neighbouring villages and convincing anyone gullible enough that he was the missing heir

The Tichborne estates remained in the possession of Roger's younger brother Alfred, until his death, and then were held in trust for his young son. The rest of the Dowager's family did not accept that Orton was in fact Roger Tichborne.

---

147   Kenealy and The Tichborne Cause – Michael Roe

In 1866 the Dowager died and Orton found that his generous allowance was no longer forthcoming. He was soon penniless and hence brought an action, in 1871, for the recovery of the Tichborne estate. The Trustees of the estate had not been idle, and had steadily accumulating information regarding Orton.

The court case, one of the longest in the English system's history, occupied one hundred and two days. During the trial the Trustees produced much evidence and witnesses. They proved that on Orton's arrival in London he had visited Wapping and inquired after the Orton family, and that members of that family had been given sums of money from him. Orton's handwriting and atrocious spelling were compared favourably to letters written by Orton to his old girlfriend in Wapping.

Evidence was taken in South America and in Australia and eventually Orton was non-suited, arrested and tried for perjury.[148]

Interesting isn't this? However, you are probably wondering what all this had to do with me. Simple, Orton was an old crony of mine. Just about all my old acquaintances from my Mewburn Park days gave evidence to the Tichborne Commission.

At Webb's Hotel on the 13th May 1869 James Andrews gave his evidence. He explained that he was a sawyer by trade and that in 1855 he was engaged by Mr Guesdon, in Tasmania, to go to Mr Johnson's at Mewburn Park, which I have already told you was situated in Gipp's Land. Andrews testified that he had arrived in Port Albert about September 1855. He had travelled on the schooner "Eclipse" and had been accompanied by only one other man called Bristol Jack. He explained that the journey from Hobart took about a week and that although he was engaged to

---

148 Australian Encyclopedia – Grolier Society of Australia, 1958.

work for Johnson for six months, he had words with Johnson and left after three months.

Andrews stated that there were about thirty to forty men on the station, he could recall a man called Arthur the butcher, but he was unable to recall his surname, he also stated that before he left Johnson's I was already employed there as a stockrider. After his departure from Mewburn Park Andrews moved around the colony of Victoria until in January 1857 he and his wife arrived in Omeo. He claimed that " I went up there to dig: when I got there Nielsen came up and Toke; there were two men with them; one they called Chapman and the other Billy the Groom; I cannot say there was any one else with them: I cannot say how long these men worked together; there was another man came the same time, a constable named Haines, and a foreigner; The Foreigner was working with Haines; I believe he afterwards worked a fortnight with me: the man I had in the pit left; so I took The Foreigner and learnt him....I should take the foreigner to be about 7 or 8 and twenty; when I left he was still there; I have seen him several times over at Nielsen's Chapman's and Toke's; there was no distance between the places; Nielsen's and Toke's party had two horses with them; one was a black horse, the other an iron-grey...I never, to my knowledge heard of Ballaarat Harry; I did not know a Ballaarat Harry, a mate of Toke's; they lived higher up the river than me: I never heard from him where he came from....he spoke as good English as I do, I never heard him speak a foreign language; I have seen him reading a book: I can't say I ever saw him write".

Alexander Nielsen also gave evidence on that day. He explained that he had travelled from Hobart Town to Mewburn Park, then commonly called Flodden Creek, on the "Eclipse" and that he had been employed there as a carpenter. Nielsen stated that he lived in the men's hut, about three hundred yards from Mr Johnson's house and that along with many others Arthur Orton and I were working and residing in the hut with him. Whilst at Mewburn Park Nielsen stated that a party of two arrived on horseback, one was Thomas Chapman and the other a young man who went by the name of The Foreigner and who had his own horse, which was iron grey in colour.

Nielsen also found his way to Omeo, in the company of Haines the former police officer, and went on to say that the first persons he saw when he reach the Livingstone Creek was me, Chapman, Billy the Groom and The Foreigner. Nielsen continued his testimony by stating that " Toke was my mate; The Foreigner never joined me; he was a partner with Toke, Chapman and Robertson; when I arrived in the evening, and they asked me to stay with them. In the morning The Foreigner had some words with Toke, and said he would not work with them any more: ... there was a horse named Charcoal; that was the iron gray belonging to The Foreigner, and a black horse called Prince, belonging to Thomas Toke; The Foreigner sold the iron grey to Mr Toke; when I left the Omeo diggings I left The Foreigner there; I then returned to Mewburn Park and saw Johnson, and again entered his service; Orton was not there when I went back..."

William Hopwood, a fencing man, stated that he had known me from my days at Mewburn Park and then at Omeo, where he confirmed that I kept an accommodation house. Alexander Arbuckle, surgeon and coroner for North Gipps Land stated "I knew Mewburn Park Station; I would know the stockriders' names if I heard them; in 1854 there were four of five stockmen at Mewburn Park; McIntosh was a stockrider, then he was overseer afterwards; I do not remember a man named Nielsen; I remember Luckman, a stockrider: I remember Toke, a notorious bushranger, then in Johnson's employ:"

The Tichborne Case

All this talk about the people at Mewburn Park and the speculation as to who "The Foreigner" was, was further enhanced when William Foster the superintendent of the station called Dargo, gave evidence to the effect that Arthur Orton had told him he could not bear the loneliness of Dargo since the murder of a man well known locally as Ballaarat Harry.

Even Henry Dickens' gave evidence, he of course confirmed that he had resided at Livingstone Creek from 1856 to 1861 and that I was well known to him, and of course he couldn't help but mentioned that I was known as a bushranger!

With the Australian and South American evidence completed by 1869, the proceedings commenced in England. At the conclusion of the trial all of the salient facts of the life of Arthur Orton had been investigated. It was proved that Orton was the son of a butcher, George Orton, born at Wapping, London, on the 20th March 1834. Orton had left school early and had been employed in this father's shop until in 1848 he was apprenticed to Captain Brooks of the ship "Ocean". The ship sailed to South America, however Orton deserted in June 1849, living in Melipilla, Chile for a year and seven months. He returned to London as an ordinary seaman and in November 1852 sailed for Tasmania, arriving in Hobart in May 1853. In 1855 Orton had taken the schooner "Eclipse" to Mewburn Park and worked in Gipps Land for approximately seven years. In 1862 he moved to Wagga Wagga, New South Wales and was employed as an assistant to a butcher and was calling himself Thomas Castro.

Arthur Orton

Having been found guilty of perjury Orton was sentenced to fourteen years penal servitude. He was a model prisoner and was released ten years later. Orton continued to call himself Sir Roger Tichborne until his dying day, the 1st April (April Fools Day) 1898.

The Tichborne mystery deepened after the conviction of Arthur Orton. There was in particular much speculation as to the possible identity of the heir, particularly in the colonies of Victoria and New South Wales. The question on most people's lips was, if Orton was not the Tichborne heir who was? The populace reasoned that Orton had had some way of obtaining information about Roger Tichborne. The accepted theory, in the colonies, was that Ballaarat Harry might have been Tichborne. After Harry's murder, it was generally believed that Orton had ransacked his belongings and found papers that indicated that Harry was the heir. A fit of guilt had made Orton fearful of returning to Ballaarat Harry's campsite on the Dargo Plains afterwards.

The authorities in Victoria had long since suspected that Ballaarat Harry was an educated young man of some standing. It was with this in mind that so many of the Australian witnesses were questioned about me, Ballaarat Harry and the horses that were in Harry's possession (the details in respect of the horses harked back to the Inquest held in 1858). I suppose the authorities considered that it was too much of a coincidence that I had worked with Orton at Mewburn Park, that Orton, like so many of my acquaintances was a butcher, and of course that he had taken up residence in Wagga Wagga, as had my butcher friends John Paynter and his brother-in-law Sidney Penny.

By the time that the Commission was conducted in Australia, I had been released from Pentridge Prison. I could have given evidence, although I doubt that I would have been believed. I could have at least set them straight as to the identity of Ballaarat Harry. I have already told you that Harry was Walter Henry Clare and that he emigrated, from Kent and arrived in South Australia in 1846. In the early 1850's Clare had brought his brother James out to Australia. James Clare lived in Omeo for many years. He too was not asked to give evidence by the Commission.

I have no idea as to whether Roger Tichborne survived the shipwreck off the coast of South America, nor do I care. Tichborne was just another example of the English gentry, a young gentleman, with too much money, a title and too many privileges who did not have the common sense to look after his best interest. Tichborne's mother was a greater fool. She obviously aided and abetted Orton's claim to the title by refusing to believe that she could be duped and that her son had survived the wreck of the "Bella".

I never credited Arthur Orton with the brains to carry off such a deception. I admired his cunning, which only shows that a foul and his money are easily parted. Unfortunately Arthur did not have long to enjoy the high-life, but still he succeeded albeit for a short time only.

Pentridge and Beyond

As I have already told you in December 1863 I was housed in Pentridge Prison. Of course I was not a model prisoner, I would never bow down to authority. However, I knew how the system worked and with my natural guile was able to ensure that I did not come under the prison authorities scrutiny too often.

I, like all inmates of Pentridge was subject to a review on a six monthly basis. In total nine half-yearly reports were recorded on my record. My behaviour on each report was noted as "good". Few misdeamours were also noted and all of these were extremely minor offences. On the 26th February 1864 I received three days solitary confinement for having a filthy closet, on the 8th October 1866 I was reprimanded for having coffee in my possession. I received three days solitary confinement on the 6th February 1867 for passing an axe to a civilian and finally on the 20th February 1867 I was convicted of passing tools out of the prison and received a further seven days solitary confinement.

I did not find it difficult to endure the punishments. It was nothing like the punishments meted out to me in Port Arthur, Norfolk Island and Carter's Barracks. I did not even complete my seven years sentence. I was discharged on the 29th June 1868, having served only four years and eight months of my sentence and was sent on my way with one day's pay![149]

I wasted no time in returning to my home at the Gibbo near Omeo. I was fifty-seven years old, as strong as an ox, highly identifiable with my misshapen arm and nose, numerous scars and tattoos and with a reputation as the area's most infamous bushranger. For your edification the definition of a bushranger in my day was a person who stole horses. I think I could safely say that I fitted the definition perfectly.

However, I had had time to reflect whilst in Pentridge and even I could see that the rough and ready days of prospecting were over.

I had yet another reason to reflect on my future. Since my enforced period of absence from my home, Ellen had taken her leave. I have not mentioned her, as she was nothing but a nagging, whining, complaining bitch. Who did she think she was marrying after all? She knew where I lived and she knew how I made my living, she should have known better than to think that she could influence or change me.

Ellen and I had not been living together for some time, she had her own place at Snowy Creek and I had my establishment. Apart from the convenience of stabling horses at my wife's place, without some nosey person asking inconvenient questions, Ellen had long since served her purpose.

Ellen Frances Toke had never been an endearing character, even Mr Foster complained about her when he made a rare visit to her home on Boxing Day 1862. Foster's description of Ellen, that she was a "loquacious and most wearing woman"[150] was a most generous description.

---

149 Toke's Prison Record.
150 Mr Foster's Diary

I have no idea as to whether Ellen had decided to leave because of my latest conviction or whether she thought it would be convenient to leave if I was not in the vicinity. If she thought that I would have tried to prevent her from leaving, well she really did not know how little I cared about her. She had long since worn out her welcome. If Ellen had been a man I would probably have considered disposing of her in a similar manner to that of Green, Davis and Ballaarat Harry. Well I was spared all of that and could contemplate my future in silence. From then on there would be me, and my dogs and to hell with the rest of the human race.

Since my incarceration the population of Omeo and surrounding goldfields had increased dramatically, there were now over three hundred European miners and more than two hundred Chinese in the area. The population of Wombat Creek was nearly two hundred and Swift's Creek, Tambo River and Livingstone Creek were no longer secluded mining towns. The Chinese threatened to outnumber the Europeans as once settled on the fields they sent for the kith and kin in China to join them.

I did not wish to return to the life of a miner, it was a dam hard life, and my reputation would prevent me from exploiting other avenues that may have appealed to many in the Colony. I therefore decided that it was time for me to take up a selection.

LAND

Once again I find that I have to explain to you the conditions that I lived under. From the moment I had set foot in the Colonies I had heard about squatters. A squatter was a farmer who occupied huge tracts of land, initially having no legal rights to the land but claiming it by right of being the first European in the area. The squatters ran large numbers of sheep and cattle on the land, and in time began to assume all the airs and graces of the English aristocracy and in fact were often described as "squattocracy".

Thanks to the gold rush in the early 1850's, Victoria's population had increased enormously. The majority of the diggers did not make their fortunes, but realised that the conditions in the Colony were better than those of their homelands. When they decided to quit the diggings they sought a future in towns or on the land within the Colony.

Initially the Colony of Victoria had made little effort to grow enough foodstuffs to supply her ever-increasing population. The Colony's squattocracy concentrated on pastoral pursuits. It became evident that the Colony needed a new breed of farmers who would produce grains, fruit and vegetables.

The squattocracy considered it their right to hold the land and spread beneficent influence over the people whom it employed upon their large holdings. The democratic instinct of the newcomers demanded an independent opportunity as the birthright of all who chose to work the land and reap its harvest. These people made their voices heard by forming an association called the Land Convention. The Convention consisted of eighty-eight delegates from all parts of the Colony and was initially presided over by Wilson Gray and Vice-Presidents Sir George Stephen and Michael Prendergast.

Wilson Gray was a liberally educated Irishman and a barrister. In England, from 1835 to 1838, he had served as a commissioner on the Poor Law Inquiry and was interested in the cause of the working classes, and small farmers. Gray then spent some time in America before he travelled to Victoria in 1854 to try his luck on the diggings. It was not long before he returned to his profession as a barrister in Melbourne.

Sir George Stephen

Sir George Stephen was the mainstay for the abolition of slavery. The original abolitionists Wilberforce, Clarkson, Macaulay and James Stephen had grown old and their work had not been completed. James Stephen bequeathed his passion in the cause to his son George, who became the prime mover and untiring labourer in the campaign. George Stephen was the author and manager of the campaign, which eventually lead to the abolition of slavery in the United Kingdom in 1834. In recognition of his services, George Stephen was knighted. In 1855 he followed his two sons to Victoria and at the age of sixty-one joined the Convention.

Parliamentary bill after parliamentary bill came and went, some pleased the squatters, some the ordinary folk. By 1860 Victoria had become one great field for discussion of land bills. The failure of bills caused instability in the Colony. In May 1860 a mass meeting of nearly six thousand people filled the Eastern Market, Melbourne where it was declared that every man in the country should have three things. Firstly a vote, which they all possessed; secondly, a rifle, which most had; third, a farm, which they must have and would have, even if the second item had to be used for the purpose.

The very next day, at five o'clock, a large crowd gathered around Parliament House. Wilson Gray addressed the crowd and invited them to follow him down Bourke Street to the Eastern Market. Once at the market Gray lectured the crowd on the line of conduct that they should adopt and warned against violence. After more speeches the crowd became inflamed, some wanted to return to Parliament House and expel its members, whilst others proposed to march on Toorak and hold an interview with the Governor. Eventually the crowd marched on Parliament where thirty policemen were on guard. A small body of mounted troopers, joined up with the police, and rode into the crowd. The crowd offered no resistance and dispersed. A force of thirty to forty police were then despatched to clear the streets. A series of conflicts ensued which left some civilians injured and seven constables badly wounded. Only after the Mayor of Melbourne, Dr. Richard Eades, read the Riot Act were the streets cleared.

Yet another Irishman, Charles Gavan Duffy, entered the fray. Duffy arrived in Victoria with his wife and children in 1855. He had been

Charles Gavan Duffy

the Member for New Ross in the House of Commons, from 1852 to 1855 and had been tried for treason under the Treason Felony Act and freed after five jury disagreements. Duffy had planned to practise as a barrister in Melbourne but had been persuaded instead to stand for the first parliament in the Colony of Victoria.

In 1861 Duffy became the President of the Board of Lands and Works, and brought his Land Bill forward in 1862. Duffy proposed that farms should be made available of not less than forty acres and no more than six hundred and forty acres. The selectors could either purchase the farm at once for one pound per acre or pay ten shillings per acre at first and then eight yearly payments of two shillings and sixpence per acre. Duffy also proposed a scheme of assignment by allotment with the holder to cultivate one-tenth of the land or fence it securely within the first year of occupancy. In June 1862 Duffy's Bill was passed and he let everyone know about his scheme by publishing pamphlets in Melbourne and London. Duffy proclaimed that Victoria was the workingman's paradise. The land was rich and lying under the ripening sunshine, crops would grow both in winter and summer.

Unfortunately Duffy's Act had a major flaw, the squatters found no difficulty in taking up the land by finding persons, who were known as "dummies", who would each select six hundred and forty acres, the squatter provided the money and the dummies would fulfil all the requirements set down by law. Once the dummies gained ownership of the land they sold it to the squatters.

Unsuccessful attempts were made to rectify the problems with the Act during the 1860's. It was not until February 1870 that the new Land Amendment Act came into force. This Act allowed any person over eighteen years of age, except a married woman living with her husband, to peg out and apply for an allotment of not more than three hundred and twenty acres of land. A license to occupy for three years, at two shilling a year per acre was then issued. The land had to be fenced and one-tenth part of the land cultivated within two years. At the expiration of three years the occupant could either pay fourteen shillings per acre, the balance of the full price of one pound per acre, or he could continue to hold the land at two shillings a year for each acre, with the understanding that as soon as he had paid one pound an acre in all he should received a Crown Grant. The Minister of Lands was made the sole judge as to whether the intention of the Act was being fulfilled and hence the dummy system was defeated.[151]

Victoria had altered significantly since I first inhabited the Colony. By the 1870's all large towns possessed police stations, doctors, shops, blacksmiths, churches and even newspapers. However civilisation was not able to control the forces of nature.

The climate in and around Omeo was harsh and unforgiving. The summer of 1870 was a particularly hot and dry one. The Chinese, of which there were increasing numbers, worked alluvial mines. Alluvial gold as distinct from reef or quartz gold is distributed through the gravels and is concentrated above the bedrock or clay. A large quantity of water

---

151 Victoria and its metropolis, past and present – Alexander Sutherland – Chapter 23 The Era of Agriculture

Above and below: Thomas Toke's land selection

Arrow indicates Toke's land

is required to wash the gold free from the dirt with a pan. By March of 1870 the alluvial mining on Swift's Creek was suspended because of the dry weather. The miners abandoned their claims and took up new ones on Livingstone Creek where there was no lack of water. A silence fell over Swift's Creek, the chatter of the Chinese was never to be heard again. The bush slowly covered the debris of twenty years of mining.

No sooner had we recovered from the drought of 1870 than we were hit with massive floods. Numerous major waterways have their origins in the High Plains all of which are fed by the snow that covers Mt. Hotham, Mt Bogong and the like. In the springs of 1870 and 1871 we experienced very heavy rainfall, this coupled by the melting snow brought floods as far afield as south Gipps Land. In mining communities in and around my neck of the woods the floods filled claims. Miners tools, pumps and wheels were buried, their boxes and flumes carried away and all the lower races were filled up or totally obliterated. Floodwaters swept away tons of tailings that clogged rivers and creeks.

The old ways were swept away by natural disaster and progress. Companies and co-operatives took the place of the single miner. Companies such as the Pioneer Claim were not new, but their techniques became more complicated and efficient.

The Pioneer Claim, which was a co-operative, had its origins back in 1858 when Edward D'Arcy Fitzgerald, George Hamilton and Duncan McCrae were all working Dry Gully. They had gained experience working the American goldfields and reasoned that by working together they could gain access to much greater areas of ground. They took up claims at the Junction of Livingstone Creek with Dry Gully and Mountain Creek. Eventually the Pioneer Claim was able to manipulate the water rights in the area and by 1873 was able to alter the operations from box sluicing to hydraulic ground and box sluicing. This process consisted of bringing large quantities of water onto an area and by directing the water by high-pressure hoses onto a suitable ore bearing face. In layman's terms this meant that they could work much larger quantities of dirt.

The Pioneer Claim was followed in 1876, by another co-operative known as the Oriental Sluicing Company. It's five shareholders were George France, Zepherim Champagne, Gilbert Hadden, Christopher Rodgers and Clarke. The company purchased twenty-five acres and leased two areas of thirty-four acres and was situated between Mountain Creek and Livingstone Creek.[152]

At the close of the 1870's Victoria had become a prosperous, sophisticated colony. It had been enriched by gold and with the influx of immigrants

---

152 Gippsland Gold Discovery – www.gippslandinfo.com.au

had turned into a major supplier of grains. With the opening up of the huge expanses of land to the ordinary folk, the Colony's primary industries were the envy of the Commonwealth. Railways, newspapers, education and modern inventions swept away the past. I could no longer live the life of seclusion that I had cherished for so long. Even small communities like Omeo and Mitta Mitta (formerly Snowy Creek) were no longer isolated. Large towns, such as Beechworth had always been within my reach. However Beechworth by 1879 boasted fine hotels, schools, banks, a railway station, telegraph office and post office.

I was about to enter my seventies, a ripe old age and one could almost say remarkable considering my background. As much as I regretted it, it was obvious I would have to alter my ways if I was to survive. My hut on the Gibbo was no longer patronised. Supplies were easily acquired in the townships at a cheaper rate. I was too old to continue mining and I could not compete with the hordes of Chinamen and the many companies with their fine new equipment.

Even my reputation as a bushranger, had been overshadowed by the infamous Ned Kelly. What did he know about bushranging? The police had come knocking on my door pleading with me to show them the passes through the mountains that my horse-thieving cronies and I had discovered in the 1850's. They were concerned the Kelly Gang would use the routes to pass undetected from the Colony of New South Wales to Victoria. I showed the police our passes, as we were long past using them for nefarious business and, because I had no time for Kelly and his gang. Even at my ripe old age, I had more cunning and guile than Ned Kelly. If the man had any sense whatsoever he would never have killed policemen. Anyone with the slightest amount of intelligent would have known that if you killed a police officer in cold blood the police force would not rest until you were captured and hung. I also had no time for the excuses Kelly made. His Irish background and his treatment by the police was nothing compared to mine treatment. I had suffered a lifetime of punishment and harassment and it made no difference that I was in fact English and Church of England.

The only amusement I gained out of the whole Kelly saga was when Sir Redmond Barry tried Kelly. I had no time for the Honourable Judge and whether it was true or not, Kelly was reported to have said to Barry " I'll see you in hell", and within days of Kelly hanging Barry was dead. That suited me fine. Barry was no longer able to remind officialdom of my past. Kelly was dead and I, many years his senior was still alive!

Mr Thomas Toke Landowner

I had begun to examine the prospects of taking up a selection in the vicinity of Omeo. It was rather ironic I thought, that if I did avail myself of the opportunity I could become a landowner just like my wealthy relatives back in Kent, England. Albeit, I would be a small landowner, but still it would be my land to use as I pleased.

I had resided in the vicinity of Omeo for nigh on thirty years and knew the land better than anyone. I had my eye on a choice piece of land and I knew how to use it. Consequently on the 26th March 1884, and in my seventy-third year, I Thomas Toke, grazier of Mitta Mitta, applied for a licence of three hundred and twenty acres in the Parish of Ludrickmunjie County of Bogong. My selection abutted the Mitta Mitta River close to Nine Mile Creek and run alongside the track to the township of Wombat. The soil was fair and the land undulating, not hilly. My selection was lightly timbered with White Gum and Peppermint trees. I gladly paid the initial sum of one pound and looked forward to my selection being surveyed and my licence being formalised.

Thomas Roudknight, Licensed Assistant Surveyor, drew up the plan of my selection, which turned out to measure three hundred and nineteen acres, three roods and thirty-one perches exactly.

My application for a Licence came before the Local Land Board at Omeo on the 28th April 1884 and naturally the granting of my licence was postponed. There were no objections, but the Board had not received the customary report from the Mines Department. I should not have felt so angry, wasn't I used to delays and adjournments? Every dammed legal proceeding I had even been involved with, in my long and colourful life had been subject to some form of delay.

I could not help but feel frustrated, I had settled my pack of dogs and my horses on my selection and I only wished to be left to my land and my isolation. I told myself that I could wait until the 23rd June to obtain a licence. It was but a short time.

On the 23rd June 1884 I once again travelled into Omeo to hear the outcome of my application. In many respects I was now feeling my age. Old scars and injuries gave me nothing but gyp in the cold, harsh winter weather. Nor did I take kindly to undertaking unnecessary trips into town. Yet again there was a further postponement! I found the paper-shuffling authorities to be unbearable, however if I was to obtain a licence for my selection I had to play their game. And so it was not until Monday the 11th August 1884 that my application for my licence was approved! I paid the initial eight pounds on the licence itself and the fee for the licence of five shillings, willingly. Notification of my licence appeared in the Government Gazette on the 12th December 1884 at page 3521 to be precise.

You must be wondering what my plan for my selection entailed. Well it had nothing to do with horses. I have told you many times before that I was a canny fellow, and I had come up with an infallible plan for my land. My selection was protected from the harsh weather by hills and some inclines, there was little vegetation and the soil was by far the best in the area. I was in fact in the possession of the only land for miles around that could establish an orchard and supply fresh fruit to Omeo and the surrounding towns. From the instant that I began to supply produce to Omeo I was made, as there was no easy way of transporting fresh produce from the traditional markets in and around Melbourne to the Omeo district in the winter months. Even during the warmer months the produce would be spoilt before it could reach such a remote area.

I had already become a common sight at the Omeo races selling fruit in 1877, a trial run so to speak. By 1884 I was selling fresh produce grown on my own land to folks who had no idea of my past history.

Around about that time I had also, for the first time in my long life, made a firm friend, a young Dane, Christian Larsen. Larsen had recently been married to a lass called Margaret. Christian, in particular enjoyed hearing my stories of the gold rush and the like, I did not feel the need to enlighten him on my personal past history as this may have had an effect on our friendship.

Christian had his own stories too. He was a giant of a young man and regularly regaled the tale of how he had set off from home to travel to the New World, and how pirates had taken his ship. Christian claimed that being so large, the pirates did not have manacles large enough to chain him and so he was able to escape and make his way to the Colony of Victoria. Whether the tale was true I can't say, but who was I to question a chap's past?

Now, according to the law, to retain my selection that I so dearly loved, I was obliged to make improvements to the land. I had initially erected a one-room log hut measuring sixteen feet by twelve feet, and had commenced fencing my property. Never an idle man, even at my age, I had continued to rise early, normally before dawn and accompanied by my dogs walked around my selection. I had great plans, there remained a lot of clearing to be done, and even after my orchard was fully established I could foresee that I would have my work cut out for me. This was the first time in my life that I truly felt contented.

Unfortunately my contentment was not to last for long. One morning in the early autumn of 1886 I rose early as usual and began my daily chores. I do not know what transpired next, only that I awoke as if from a long sleep and found myself lying on the ground by my hut with my faithful dogs by my side. Try as I may I could not get up and lay on the spot until I was eventually found by Christian Larsen.

I was horrified to find that when Christian asked me what ailed me I could not speak. I became very agitated and even though I was aware that Christian was concerned about my well being my aggressive nature bubbled to the surface. I could not lash out, one whole side of my body was paralysed and all I could do was passively watch as the giant Dane carefully lifted me onto his wagon and drove me to his home.

When Margaret Larsen set eyes on me, she immediately began to order her kind-hearted husband about. Telling him to be gentle with the old man! Old man I shouted in my brain, I'm not a feeble old man, I am Thomas Toke bushranger. Show some respect! But not a word came out of my mouth.

The Larsen's set about to make me comfortable in their home and did show me more kindness than any other human beings had done in my seventy-five years. Christian cared for his selection and mine, and each evening would tell me what he had done that day and that soon I would return to my selection and finish planting my fruit trees and fencing the property.

I felt like I was in prison again. At first I told myself that it was just like solitary confinement and I would endure the cursed bout of illness. However the seasons and the months rolled by and my health and my humour did not improve.

Margaret Larsen had at first complained that I was filthy, so I may have been, but did it matter? I had only to please myself and I did not see the need to trouble myself with weekly washes or regular changes of clothes. Clothing was expensive and no amount of fashionable clobber would have altered my looks, and I certainly had not seen the need to impress the townsfolk of Omeo.

In accordance with Margaret's wishes my clothes were burnt and I was subjected to humiliating and regular washes. Margaret knew I did not approve, she only needed to look into my eyes as they flashed with anger. There was no other form of communication between us and although I had lost the power of speech there was still nothing wrong with my reasoning or my hearing.

Margaret had not travelled into town on a regular basis during the winter months of 1886. The track to town was either covered in snow or wet, boggy and unpassable. Nothing remained dry, it was cold and dreary and from my sick bed the world had become remote and the days never-ending. When spring eventually arrived and Margaret began to travel into town and hence gossip with her lady friends, she returned home and told Christian alarming stories that she had heard about me.

According to the folks around about, and I must point out none of them had lived anywhere near as long as I had in the vicinity, I was supposed to be a gypsy and had murdered at least seven miners. I was said to have hacked my victims to deaths, burnt their bodies and thrown their bones down abandoned mine shifts. The stories angered me, they were patent lies or at the very least gross exaggerations. Nevertheless I knew that Margaret believed these tales. Even though I could not lift a finger against her I knew that Margaret was no longer willing to care for me.

Eventually Margaret had her way and Christian loaded me up onto his wagon and drove me all the way to Beechworth, where I was admitted to the Ovens District Hospital. I remembered little of my last few months of life. Long and eventful as my life had been, I received no visitors and no recognition for my past fame. Even before I died it was as if my part in history had been completely eradicated, like most aged and ailing folk I was almost totally ignored. On the 27th July 1887 I died. It was a peaceful death, I had cheated the gallows and out-lived all of my contemporaries. I managed to simply die of old age.

I was buried in the Beechworth Cemetery at 3.00pm within the Church of England section. The Reverend Charles Payne presided, even though no one attended my funeral. A wooden headstone was erected and as my body was laid to rest the facts of my life began to blur and fade. My headstone and my Death Certificate referred to me as Thomas "Toake", my age at death was put at eighty-eight years. I have never spelt my name as "Toake" and I was only seventy-six years old.[153]

The day after my death the Ovens and Murray Advertiser reported my death by simply stating:

---

153 Toke's Death Certificate – 1887, No.9133

Mr Thomas Toke Landowner

TOAKE – At the Ovens District Hospital, on the 27th July 1887, Thomas Toake, late of Mitta Mitta, aged 88 years. 27 days in the hospital".

A small article also appeared which commenced with the statement that:

"many queer stories were in circulation regarding Toake's career thirty years ago, his name being connected with the disappearance of two or three men in the Mitta Mitta district who were supposed to have been robbed and murdered"[154]

---

154 Ovens and Murray Advertiser 29 July 1887

The Aftermath of Toke's Death

I told you that I embraced the law in my old age! I even went to the trouble of writing a Will. I expect you want to know who benefited under its provisions. Well the details were as follows:

"I Thomas Toke late of

Mitta Mitta Farmer

This is the last Will and Testament of me Thomas Toke made this 26th day of September One thousand eight hundred and eighty, as follows I give devise and bequeath all my furniture ready money goods and chattels and all other my real and personal estate and effects whatsoever unto my dear friend Christian Larsen his heir's executors administrators and to and for his own absolute use and benefit according to the nature and quality thereof respectively subject only to the payment of my just debts funeral and testamentary expenses and the charges of proving and registering this my Will. And I appoint Christian Larsen executor

Thomas Toke's will and testament

The Aftermath of Toke's Death

of this my Will, and hereby revoke all other Wills. In Witness whereof I have hereunto set my hand the day and year above, written _____

_____ Thomas Toke_____(Seal)____ Signed published and acknowledged by the said Thomas Toke as and for his last Will and Testament in the presence of us, who in his presence and at his request and in the presence of each other have subscribed our names as Witnesses_____Witnesses_____

___James Aitken ___Hansen Peter Jensen __Hans Otto _"[155]

I had informed Christian that he was to be the sole beneficiary under my Will, and I expect that he thought that it would be a simple matter to wind up my affairs, but as was the case with anything I had a hand in, this was not to be.

As you know my selection was a choice one, and since me death, there was much speculation as to what Christian planned to do with the land. I doubt that Christian had expected a battle to retain the land, firstly as my executor and secondly as the beneficiary. Unfortunately he was soon to find himself in a legal wrangle over my land.

On the 20th January 1888 Richard Gill wrote a spiteful letter to the Secretary of Lands in Melbourne, in which he applied for my selection. Gill contended that I had not complied with the Land Act in any reasonable way. Gill wrote:

> ".. he has never been on the land since it has been applied ...I was well acquainted with him I have not seen him in the district for the last six months, to my knowledge the block is unoccupied. Joseph Bilton makes use of it occasionally for grazing purposes. Sir I would be

---
[155] Toke's Will dated September 26, 1880

thankful if you would comply with my request to have it thrown open. I would take it and a position on the Back for 640 acres, there is 50 acres more or less fit for cultivation with very little clearing for which I would be glad of as I have not much land on my selection to cultivate as I have a great idea of putting in a large orchard. Toke's block would serve me well as it is a far warmer climate than here in Hinno Munjie, for further information reply as soon as possible".

All lies of course, if Gill knew me so well he would have been aware that I had been dead for six months and could not have been occupying my land. The truth of the matter was that he had always coveted my selection and took the opportunity to try to take Larsen's legacy by blatant lies and misrepresentations.

Gill's application instigated much correspondence between the Lands Department in Melbourne and the authorities in Omeo. Mr Foster, the Bailiff at Omeo, was instructed by the Lands Department to address the accusations made by Gill. Foster confirmed that I had died in Beechworth Hospital some six months ago and that a number of improvements were on my selection including:

> One hundred and seventy chains of log fence, amounting to the value of eighty-five pounds;
>
> Six chains of post and three rails, amounting to six pounds;
>
> Ringing amounting to the value of twenty pounds and,
>
> Clearing of the land amounting to ten pounds.
>
> The total of the improvements to the land estimated to be one hundred and one pounds worth.

The Aftermath of Toke's Death

Joseph Bilton, a local grazier supported Christian Larsen's claim to the land.

Christian, who had a very good hand and a way with words, wrote to his Member of Parliament, Peter Wright, requesting that he "kindly call on the Minister of Lands and explain how it was that Toke did not reside on the lands, as you know he stopped with me all through his illness, and when he died left me all his property etc also his selection with improvements to the extent of two hundred and sixty pounds and sixteen shillings and I am quite prepared to pay all rents and comply with all conditions".[156]

Peter Wright did in fact forward Christian's letter to the Office of Lands and Survey Melbourne, and also supported his claim to my selection.

Probate on my estate, was granted to Christian Larsen on the 4th April 1888 and no more objections in respect of my selection were made. Mind you, I doubt that I would have relied totally on the local authorities to see off my competition. If I had been alive I am sure I would have made Richard Gill pay dearly for his attempt to obtain my land under false pretences.

On the 25th September 1891 Christian applied for a lease of my selection. He was also able to declare that as the Executor of my Estate he had, paid ninety-six pounds being all fees due on the licence, fenced the whole property within two years of the issue of the licence, erected a one room log hut with a bark roof, built a stockyard, cleared the scrub and picked up all dead timber on the land. The total cost of the improvements to my

---

156   Larsen's letter dated March 17, 1888

land amounted to three hundred and twenty-five pounds, two shillings and six pence.[157]

Yes, but there were to be more delays! The Secretary for the Office of Lands and Survey in Melbourne wrote to Christian:

"Referring to your application for lease of the land I beg to inquire if the late licensee complied with the conditions of his license prior to his death".[158]

Once again Christian was forced to explain the circumstances surrounding my death. Luckily he was a good-natured man. I would not have taken the repeated questioning and continual delays in confirming my right to my land, without some reprisal on a petty bureaucrat.

Eventually, on the 19th January 1892, the lease of my land, for a period of fourteen years, was granted to Christian Larsen. Christian had had enough of my land by this stage and on the 1st June 1892 transferred the leasehold of my selection to Joseph Bilton, grazier of Omeo.

With the passing of my selection to Bilton there should have been few persons in the Colony of Victoria who would have cause to remember me. This was not to be. You would have thought that the murders of Ballaarat Harry and Cornelius Green should have faded into oblivion, but no, they were to surface once more.

A book, entitled "Nevermore" written by Judge Thomas Alexander Browne, under the penname of Rolf Boldrewood, was published in 1892. Now if you are astute you should be asking yourselves why the name Browne is familiar to you? If not I will explain. Judge Browne's

---

[157] Application for Lease by Licensee of Land Under "The Land Act 1869" as Amended by "The Land Act 1878".
[158] Secretary, Office of Lands and Survey to Christian Larsen 3rd October 1891.

father, Sylvester Browne, was a member of the jury that had found me guilt of horse stealing in 1841.

Judge Browne's sister was the wife of Judge Moleworth, who of course presided over the initial Chamberlain and Armstrong trial. Could I ever escape the attention of this family?

The coincidences continued, as Sylvester Browne had lost his immense fortune in the "black forties" when prices fell, and cash became scarce. All Browne's Melbourne town lots were lost in this crash. His large property, "Darlington", situated in the foothills of Mount Macedon, was divided and sold. Half of the property which including ten thousand sheep, was acquired by a gentleman named Thomas Baynton. Judge Robert Pohlman, the presiding Judge in the second Chamberlain and Armstrong trial, purchased the other half of the property.[159]

The book, "Nevermore " was set in and around Omeo and concerned the murders of Ballaarat Harry and Cornelius Green. The details of the death of Cornelius Green were far removed from the facts. According to the book, Green and party were travelling by coach when they were ambushed. "Nevermore" was a highly romantic Victorian novel, which was a total failure. I cannot say that this would have upset me, Browne should have kept himself to his profession and left the likes of me alone.

---

159 Old Melbourne Memories – Rolf Boldrewood.

Thomas Toke's death certificate

The Twentieth Century

In 1918 ex-Mounted Trooper William Greene, aged 81, the sole surviving member of Cornelius Greene's party gave an interview to The Leader Newspaper. Greene provided his account of Cornelius Green's murder and stated that the Victorian Government had awarded him two years' leave on full pay after he was wounded in the incident. Initially he had returned to the Old Country to see his folks and then went off to New Zealand when the gold rushes opened there. With Sergeants Bracken and Sheridan, and under Commissioner St.John Brannigan, Greene had formed a gold escort there. Altogether Greene claimed that he was a policeman for forty-three years.

Greene was residing at Moonambel, twelve miles from Avoca, at the time of his interview, but had come down to meet one of his sons, Private Albert Charles Greene M.M. on his return from the battlefields of France at the end of World War One.

It is fitting that I provide you with the details of Greene's sons, as they like myself form an integral part of British, Australian and Victoria's history.

Albert Charles Greene, aged twenty-five, born at Moonammbel, in Victoria, enlisted in the 8th Infantry Battalion, which was raised from rural Victoria by Lieutenant Colonel William Bolton at the time of the declaration of the First World War. The Battalion formed part of the 2nd Brigade.

The 2nd Brigade, including Private Albert Charles Greene, service number 891, took part in the ANZAC landing on the 25th April 1915, as part of the second wave. Ten days after, the 2nd Brigade was transferred from ANZAC to Cape Helles to aid in the attack on Krithia. The Brigade lost almost a third of its strength. After the withdrawal from Gallipoli the Battalion returned to Egypt and in March 1916 it sailed to France and the Western Front. From then until 1918 the Battalion was heavily involved in action against the German Army. In 1917 the Battalion joined the great offensive launched to the east of Ypres.

> "During the attack on Polygon Wood east of Ypres on September 20th 1917 when the position had been captured and consolidated this man (Private Albert Charles Greene) went along to the right flank and took up a position in an advanced strong point and with his machine gun picked off the enemy who were attempting to counterattack at this point. By his coolness and courage he probably saved the whole flank from falling in action"[159]

Private Albert Charles Greene was awarded the Military Medal and after the end of World War One returned home with the remnants of his Battalion.

Greene, had another son who served in the First World War, he was Private Percival Ernest Greene, later promoted to Lance Corporal. At the

---

[159] Private Albert Charles Greene citation for the Military Medal

age of twenty-six Percival enlisted in the 14th Battalion in Moonambel on the 31st August 1914. With the 13th, 15th and 16th Battalions, the 14th formed the 4th Brigade commanded by John Monash.

Percival Ernest Greene, number 5380, embarked on the 4th April 1916 on HMAT Eurpides and joined the 4th Brigade in Egypt after the Brigade had suffered heavy causalities defending the ANZAC front line. In June 1916 the 4th Brigade sailed for France and the Western Front. The Brigade's first action in France was at Pozieres in April 1917. The Battalion suffered heavy losses at Bullecourt. During this battle Lance Corporal Percival Ernest Greene, aged 29, was killed. He was laid to rest at the Cemetery at Villers Bretonneux, France.[160]

So, just as no one remembered my contribution to Victoria's history, I imagine that few of you knew about the Greene family's contribution either.

Life goes on you my say, and with the course of time, I was just a memory to the old folks of the Omeo area. No one visited my grave in Beechworth and in fact after the bush fires of the 1930's that swept right through that area, and claimed my wooden headstone, there was no tangible link left with my life.

A century after my death the only reference to me was a place called "Toak's Gibbo". What an insult, once again my name was spelt wrongly! The site is situated to the north of Omeo and I think that I am owed at least the right to have the place re-named "Toke's Gibbo"! Perhaps after you have read my life's history you may feel that you have an obligation to once again bring my name to the attention of the authorities and have this final injustice remedied.

---

[160] Australian War Memorial Roll of Honour.

Conclusion

Thomas Toke

So now you know my history. I, Thomas Toke, played an integral part in the early history of Australia. You never knew I existed and in your ignorance believed that Ned Kelly was a "great" bushranger. He was a flash in the pan. I was the true bushranger. I was the one who survived the harsh punishments meted out to the dregs of English society. I was the one who suffered in the hellholes at Carter's Barracks, Port Arthur and Norfolk Island. I endured the lash and solitary confinement and I forged the tracks into the vast and unknown bush of Victoria. You forgot, or chose not to learn about the past, shame on you!

Heed my words well, never accept popular opinion as fact, never accept complacency and give thanks to the likes of me who gave you a rich and colourful heritage to cherish. You are now the custodian of early Victorian history, do not banish it yet again to the dusty shelves of libraries and the cold vaults of archives. I charge you with the responsibility of passing on our history to the next generation and remind you that if you fail to uphold my wishes, Old Thomas Toke may pay you a visit one dark, cold night!

And yes, just once in a while old cocks do crow!

INDEX

A

Albury 175
Annikie Yeo-Yang. 33
Armstrong, William 85, 109, 110, 113, 115, 117, 121, 122, 125, 140, 142, 147, 152, 157, 162, 163

B

Baigrie, Captain 14, 15
Baigrie, Mr 12
Baker, Henry 33
Ballaarat Harry. *See* Clare, Walter Henry
Ballarat 61, 62, 80, 89
Barrow, Samuel 54
Barry, Redmond 32, 187, 218
Batman, John 21
Baynton, Thomas 233
Beechworth 71, 72, 77, 78, 92, 112, 132, 171, 174, 175, 176, 179, 185, 186, 187, 190, 192, 193, 217, 224, 230, 237
Beechworth Court 175
Beechworth, HM Prison 193
Bendigo 61
Beswick, Charles 33
Billy the Groom. *See* Armstrong, William
Bird, Frederick 81
Bligh, William 56
Bogong Jack. *See* Joseph Paynter
Boldrewood, Rolf 232, 233
Boyle, Constable 29
Braithwait, Frederick 188
Brassington, George 5
Brisbane, Sir Thomas 51
Broadfoot, Alexander 32
Brown, Ebenezer 33
Browne, Emma 123
Browne, Judge Thomas Alexander 232
Browne, Sylvester John 33, 123, 233
Brown, John 33
Bryan, Reverend 163

Buckingham, George 33
Buckley, John 184
Bullivant, John 33
Bussorah Merchant 9, 12, 13, 14, 15

C

Canvas Town 60
Carters' Barracks 17
Cash, Martin 39, 42
Chamberlain, George 96, 98, 109, 110, 113, 114, 115, 116, 117, 121, 122, 140, 142, 147, 148, 152, 156, 163
Champagne, Zepherim 216
Chapman, Henry Samuel 136
Chatham 12
Cheong, Ah 177
Child, Ensign 12
Childs, Major 52
Christian, Fletcher 56
Chun, Ah 177
Clare, Walter Henry 68, 75, 77, 84, 91, 93, 102, 203
Clarke, Ellen Frances 77, 131
Clark Haines, William 135
Cobb and Co. 132, 146
Cobb, Freeman 146
Cole, Captain 27, 29
Collingwood Stockade 126, 127
Collins Street 24, 26, 33, 36, 122, 124
Colony of New South Wales 19, 181, 217
Cope, Thomas 187
Coulson, W. 32
Court of Petty Sessions 184
Cox, Francis James 32
Crimp, William 152
Criterion Hotel 183
Crockett, A. 33
Croke, James 31
Cummins, John 32

Currie Wills, Alfred 68, 81, 90
Cuthbertson Sutherland, James 46, 49

D
Dale Park 106
D'Arcy Fitzgerald, Edward 216
Dargo High Plains 68
Davies Ireland, Richard 123, 136
Davis, John. *See* John McCarty
Davis, Soames 88, 122, 125, 151, 174, 179, 180, 181
Day, Joseph 80, 109, 116, 124, 145
Day's Hotel 80, 109
DeGraves, Mr 188
Deveney, Captain 12
Dickens, Henry 111, 115, 117, 145, 148, 181, 201
Dickins, Henry 111
Diggers Arms Hotel 113
Donnybrook 26
Dore, A. 46
D'Oyley, John 8
Dry Gully 216
Duffy, Charles Gavan 136, 211, 212
Du Moulin 67
Dunn, Dr. R. 12

E
Eades, Dr. Richard 211
Eaglehawk Neck 38, 39, 40
Eardley-Wilmot, Sir John 50
Eclipse 66, 198, 199, 201
Eureka Stockade 123

F
Fainting Range 71
Falkiner, Frederick 28
Fane, Constable 88, 175
Finigan, Michael 20, 24, 27, 28, 36
Fisher, Robert James 74, 115, 168
Fitzgerald, Thomas 48
Foster Station 73, 89
France, George 216
Frury, John 48

G
George, Judge James 88
Gibbo Creek 74, 88, 107, 108, 117, 118, 149, 155, 175

Gibbo Road 188
Gibbs, William 118
Gidley King, Phillip 51
Gilligan, Constable 188
Gipps Land 21, 66, 73, 85, 89, 92, 106, 107, 124, 129, 173, 179, 200, 201, 215
Gipps, Sir George 31, 66
Godinton Park 3, 4, 5
gold 59, 60, 61, 62, 64, 71, 74, 77, 101, 106, 107, 109, 216
Golden Age Hotel Omeo 111
goldfield 61, 113
Grainger, Joseph 88
Granville. Robert 88
Gray, Wilson 210, 211
Green, Cornelius 101, 105, 106, 107, 108, 109, 110, 111, 112, 114, 115, 120, 122, 148, 149, 150, 152, 156, 160, 167, 168, 179, 181, 232, 233, 235
Greene, Mounted-Constable William 111, 115, 140, 141, 142, 147, 153, 156, 166, 168, 181, 235
Greene, Percival Ernest 236, 237
Greene, Private Albert Charles 235, 236
Greeves, Augustus 136
Guesdon, Mr 198

H
Hadden, Gilbert 216
Hamilton, Archibald 81, 85
Hamilton, George 216
Hanekar, Dejarlais 71
Hanekar, Louis 71
Hargraves, Edward 59
Hedley, Doctor 71
Hill, Henry 68, 75, 128
Hobart Town 38, 42, 45, 47, 48, 50, 54, 67, 199
Hodgson, Charles Howell 186, 191
Hodgson, John 189
Hogan, Denis 20, 24, 25
Houses of Parliament 122
Hughes, Phillip 47

J
Jack, Bristol 198
Johnson, Mr 65, 66, 198, 199
Jones, George 39

Index

Jones, John Dudley 190

K
Kavanagh, Lawrence 39
Kelly, Ned 1, 217
Keong Ah Yow, Ah 177
Kiddy, John. *See* John McCarty
Kiewa 71
King George III 45
King, Sergeant 184, 188, 189, 190
Kinlochewe Inn 24, 25, 26, 28, 124

L
Lafeber, Louis 177
Lake Crescent 47
Lamber, John B 146
Larsen, Christian 221, 222, 227, 231, 232
Larsen, Margaret 222, 223
La Trobe, Governor 60, 143
Launceston 45, 46
Livingstone Creek 69, 71, 73, 75, 77, 90, 102, 118, 147, 149, 152, 168, 170, 176, 181, 183, 184, 188, 200, 201, 207, 215, 216
Livingstone Police Station 146, 169
Loftus Lynn, Adam 184, 186, 190, 191
Logie, Mr 28, 29, 35
Logie, William 33
Lynn, Adam 185, 189, 191

M
Macalister, Mr 118
Macquarie, Governor Lachlan 45
Macquarie Springs 45
Madame Lee's Waxworks 166
Manson, Sergeant 75, 81, 82, 88
McCalaster River 73
McCarty, John 20, 24
McCrae, Duncan 216
McDonald, Annie 98
McDonald, Charles 88, 95
McGowan, John 88
McIntosh 67, 200
McMahon, John 110, 145, 146, 151, 157, 181
McMillanm Mr 73
Mechanics' Institute 188
Melbourne 23, 24, 26, 27, 28, 29, 30, 31, 32, 33, 36, 59, 60, 61, 63, 64, 66, 68, 84, 91, 106, 107, 116, 120, 121, 122, 123, 124, 126, 127, 128, 131, 132, 136, 137, 141, 142, 143, 144, 146, 151, 159, 166, 167, 168, 169, 170, 171, 172, 175, 176, 188, 192, 210, 211, 212, 221, 229, 230, 231, 232, 233
Melbourne Cemetery 166
Melbourne Gaol 36, 126
Merri Creek 26
Mewburn Park 65, 66, 67, 69, 72, 73, 198, 199, 200, 201, 202
Michie, Archibald 135
Mitta Mitta River 175, 189, 219
Molesworth, Sir Robert 122, 123, 126, 127
Montagu, Mr Justice 47, 50
Moonambel 235, 237
Moran, Adam 48
Mountain Creek 216
Mount-stephens, James 48
Muir, Sarah 120
Mutter, Eliza 111, 112, 114, 145

N
Neale, Charles 20, 24, 26
New Zealand 61, 167, 181, 235
Nicholson River 102
Nicholson, William 137
Nielsen, Alexander 199
Nine Mile Creek 219
Norfolk Island 40, 50, 51, 52, 54, 55, 56, 57, 205
Norton, Philip 73, 89

O
Oatlands 43, 44, 45, 46, 47, 57, 59
Oatlands Supreme Court 47
O'Hara Burke, Robert 187
Omeo 68, 70, 71, 72, 74, 75, 78, 80, 81, 82, 83, 84, 85, 89, 90, 91, 92, 93, 95, 98, 99, 101, 102, 103, 104, 105, 106, 107, 109, 111, 112, 113, 114, 115, 116, 119, 125, 128, 129, 132, 137, 138, 141, 160, 161, 166, 167, 168, 172, 173, 174, 175, 176, 179, 181, 183, 184, 185, 186, 187, 188, 189, 190, 191, 192, 199, 200, 203, 206, 207, 213, 217, 219, 220, 221, 223, 230, 232, 233, 237
Omeo Court House 84

Omeo Cricket Club 172
Omeo log gaol 83
Omeo Plains 116, 160, 161, 190
Oriental Sluicing Company 216
Orton, Arthur 67, 200, 201, 202, 203
Orton, George 197, 201
O'Shanassy, John 135, 136
Ovens District Hospital 224, 225

P
Pascoe Fawkner, John 21
Paynter, Joseph 66, 68, 69, 72, 145
Peck, John Murray 146
Pedrazzi, Joseph 186, 188, 189, 191, 192
Penny, Sidney 109, 114, 116, 117, 127, 148, 150, 171, 175, 181, 202
Pentridge Prison 159, 192, 202, 205
Pentridge Stockade 126, 157, 159, 163, 192, 202, 205, 206
Pepper, Senior Constable James 186
Pinchin, Joseph 88
Pioneer Claim 216
Pohlman, Judge Robert 143, 156, 157, 233
Port Arthur 37, 38, 39, 41, 42, 55, 56, 57, 58, 205
Port Phillip 21, 23, 24, 25, 26, 27, 29, 31, 34, 36, 37, 46, 60, 123, 135
Port Phillip Herald 24, 25, 26, 27, 29, 31, 34, 36

Q
Queen's Wharf 121

R
Read, Inspector 118
Robinson Uneet, James 33
Rodgers, Christopher 216

S
Sailor Jack. *See* Turner Taylor, John
Sewell, Dr 124, 143, 144, 147, 149, 151, 153, 157, 163
Sewell, Mr 26, 124
Sheean, Thomas 75, 77, 80, 81, 88, 172
smallpox 12
Snowy Creek 175, 185, 186, 189, 206, 217
Standish, Frederick 129, 169
Stephen, Frank 144, 157

Stephen, Sir George 210
Stewart, John 29
St Patrick's Day 73
Supreme Court of Victoria 143, 188
Sutton, Robert 47
Swanston, James 146
Swift's Creek 103, 109, 111, 115, 117, 120, 148, 160, 167, 207, 215
Sydney 1, 9, 12, 13, 14, 15, 17, 20, 21, 23, 25, 28, 31, 51, 159, 171, 197
Sydney Town 17, 23

T
Table Top 175
The Sea Horse 37
Tichborne, Earl of 197
Tichborne, Henriette Felicite 195
Tichborne, Orton 197
Tichborne, Roger Charles 195
Toak's Gibbo 237
Toke, Elizabeth Sarah, nee Smith 3
Toke, Ellen Frances 206
Toke, Thomas 1, 3, 75, 76, 93, 132, 186, 188, 200, 214, 219, 222, 227, 228, 229, 234, 239, 240
Tongio Hill 115
Tongio Station 117
Turner Taylor, John 82, 84, 88, 184, 185, 191

V
Van Diemen's Land 23, 37, 43, 44, 46, 47, 48, 50, 55, 56, 57, 59

W
Wagga Wagga 171, 175, 181, 197, 201, 202
Walhalla 67
Walpole Willis, Judge John 30, 31, 32, 36
Wapping 198, 201
Wells, Henry 78
Wentworth River 83, 84
Westwood, William 54, 55
Wheelers River 175
White, Constable 146, 152, 169
Whittaker, Robert 81
Williams, Joseph 88
William's Town 23
Wilson, Dr Robert 55

INDEX

Wombat 189, 207, 219
Woolaston, Jacob 80
Wright, John 153, 172, 173
Wright, Peter 231
Wright, William 23, 28

Y

Yackandandah 71, 72, 146, 174, 176, 179, 180, 186
Yackandandah Creek 179, 180
Yarra River 21, 122

www.ingramcontent.com/pod-product-compliance
Lightning Source LLC
Chambersburg PA
CBHW070732160426
43192CB00009B/1408